BOUND FOR SUCCESS

Guiding Your Child Toward Higher Self-Esteem

by
Bert Simmons

with
Betty Jo Simmons

Bert and Betty Jo Simmons would like to acknowledge the contributions of Mark Falstein (whose skill with the English language is phenomenal), Kathy Winberry and Carol Navratil in making this book what it is.

Editorial Staff
Marlene Canter
Jacqui Hook
Barbara Schadlow
Marcia Shank

Design
Carol Provisor

Cover Design
The Arcane Corporation

ISBN #0-939007-79-7

First Printing December 1993
97 96 95 94   8 7 6 5 4 3 2

This book is dedicated to
Kristina
whose mastery of the monkey bars
while in the second grade was my insipiration, and to
Mary, Sandra, John and Steve
from whom I gained the wisdom of experience.

Contents

Introduction

"Let everything you do be done as if it makes a difference," William James wrote a century ago. In none of life's experiences is his advice more vital than in bringing up children.

I'd been a parent more than 30 years before this realization fully hit home. The occasion was the birth of my second grandchild—only six weeks after the birth of my first. With both my daughters pregnant I had looked forward to grandparenthood with double anticipation, and the actuality was even more wonderful than what I had imagined. Yet now as I sat in an easy chair on my deck, I felt a different emotion. I was shivering—not from the cool breeze, but from thoughts of the awesome responsibility of parenting. I was aware that it was not only my daughters I had parented but their newborn children as well...and *their* children, and so on down the generations. What I had taught my children by deed, action, and example would now be passed along to my grandchildren.

I thought of those special times I had shared with my children—the walks we took, the quiet afternoons on our farm—and the ordinary times too. The examples I set as they were growing up constituted their most significant lessons in child rearing—and it was this reflection that made me shiver.

Had I been a positive role model for my children? Had I allowed them an appropriate measure of choice in who they wanted to be? Had I instilled in them a sense of their uniqueness and value? A commitment to responsibility? I could remember tender words I had spoken, but I could remember insensitive words too: "You know, sometimes you're a real bother." "She's the shy one, hiding behind her ol' dad." "You are so *dense* sometimes!"

In brief: How had my input as a parent impacted my children's self-esteem?

Self-Esteem: The Cornerstone of Your Child's Success

We all want our children to be successful—no matter how we may measure success. We want them to be able to take control of their lives, to find personal fulfillment in whichever ways they may choose. And during my thirty-seven years as a teacher, principal and educational consultant, my personal observations have affirmed the results of study after study: *The single most significant factor in determining a child's success is his or her self-esteem.*

"Self-esteem," wrote teacher and family therapist Dorothy Corkille Briggs, "is the mainspring that slates every child for success or failure as a human being." This is a correlation so consistent you can bank on it. Self-esteem transcends such other factors as education, economic opportunity, social group, or having a parent at home full time. A child with low self-esteem defines herself by her disappointments and failures. A child with high self-esteem shrugs off personal setbacks and identifies with her successes. And while siblings, teachers and peers play a role in influencing a child's sense of self, it is *we parents* whose input is most vital in developing this psychological self-portrait of a malleable human being—a child who will someday be an adult with children of his or her own.

> *A child with high self-esteem shrugs off personal setbacks and identifies with her successes.*

"An infant coming into this world," wrote child-development specialist Virginia Satir, "...must rely on the experiences he has with the people around him and the messages they give him about his worth as a person. For the first five or six years, the child's [self-esteem] is formed by the family almost exclusively. After he starts to school, other influences come into play, but the family remains important all through...adolescence."

We parents hold the power of life in our hands. We literally teach our children what it means to be *human*—how to think, feel and care for others, and how to express love. It is we whose actions and examples most determine whether or not our children face the world with pride, confidence, and a positive attitude toward life—and that's why I've written *Bound for Success*.

What this Book Can Do for You

Bound for Success is a collection of ideas, examples, tips and techniques for helping your children develop high self-esteem. It's a guidebook, a road map for parents who want to maximize their children's chances for success— to empower them to do and become anything they wish. Though this process requires your diligence and commitment, *Bound For Success* is designed for easy use. You can read it in one sitting or peruse it slowly, then refer back as needed to pertinent information.

Bound for Success Will Show You:

- your crucial role in developing your child's **self-esteem**, the single most significant factor in determining his or her future success.

- why your **unconditional love**, balanced with clear and specific limits, is crucial to your child's sense of self.

- how to encourage **achievement** and help your child develop the feeling of competence essential to self-esteem.

- how to guide your child in **setting goals**—a necessary pre-requisite to achievement.

- mental techniques your child can use to **banish self-doubt and build self-confidence**.

Continued

Continued

- how to encourage the **positive mental attitude** that enables your child to shake off disappointment and lets success build on success.

- how to be a **role model** for your child and guide him in choosing other role models.

- how to recognize and encourage your child's **uniqueness** and individual worthiness.

- how to develop the habit of **attentive listening** that nurtures a child's positive sense of self.

- how to teach your child **personal responsibility**.

- how to teach your child a sense of **responsibility to others**.

- how to help your child develop an **aspect of success**.

- how to help your child develop the **qualities that lead to success**.

Contributing greatly to the content and preparation of *Bound for Success* is my wife, Betty Jo Simmons. As a parent, teacher and educational consultant, she brings valuable experience and insight to the task of guiding children toward success.

We begin with a simple story of one child's success. Consider it as a fable: Though "Sarah" is based on a real person, her story has been changed somewhat to highlight a few illustrative points. As you read it, see if you can pick up on the key phrases that indicate how a series of seemingly ordinary events during the course of an ordinary week helped place a child on the path toward becoming a successful adult.

Sarah

Our level of self-esteem can often be measured by how we conduct ourselves as we go about even the most usual of daily events. Sarah was a girl whose feelings of personal worth were reflected in her thoughts and actions as she waited in the school yard for her turn on the bars.

Sarah stood in the playground waiting for her turn on the bars. Her palms were sweating. There were still three children in line ahead of her, and she wanted to practice her routine one more time before the bell rang.

As she waited, Sarah went through the routine in detail in her mind. She saw herself placing her hands just so, felt the friction of the bars against her palms as she executed each turn, timed her releases as she swung from one bar to the next, her hair flying behind her. This mental practice seemed to calm the fluttering in her stomach. "You can do it," she told herself silently. "You're as ready as you could ever be."

She had been practicing for weeks, every day before school and at lunchtime. It was a harder routine than she'd ever done before, highlighted by a one-legged twirl around the highest bar. When she'd planned it, she'd broken it down into steps. She'd practiced each one in turn until she got it right, and today was the day she'd set for putting all the steps together. She'd always enjoyed playing on the bars, but having a particular goal and a plan for reaching it seemed to focus her efforts. Now, so close to her goal, she allowed herself to think ahead to Saturday, when she would bring her parents to the playground. Were they going to be surprised!

Now Lauren was mounting the bars. Sarah watched her closely, concentrating on her every move. Lauren was the best athlete in the class. She moved with the grace and self-assurance of the gymnasts Sarah had seen on TV. When Sarah had first seen her on the bars, she hoped that she could someday be as good as Lauren, and she told her so. A week later, Sarah had been taking her turn when she noticed Lauren watching her. "You're pretty good," Lauren said after she dismounted, "but you're using your knees too much. You'd get a lot more height if you'd swing from your hips."

"From my hips?" Sarah said. "Can you show me?"

> *Sarah enjoyed the feeling that came from doing things well, from making choices and following through.*

That day they began to work together. Now Sarah wasn't particularly concerned about whether she would ever be as good as Lauren; she simply wanted to be the best she could be at something she liked. She enjoyed the feeling that came from doing things well, from making choices and following through. She thought of words like "pride" and "self-confidence," but the feeling was more than that. It was a sense of somebodiness; a sense that she was worth something—even if it was only performing on the playground bars.

Sarah stepped forward. She wiped her hands on her shorts and took a deep breath. A swift climb up the pole and she was hanging from the first bar. Now a skin-the-cat and a quick vault to the next bar. She was moving with the ease of a circus performer. She did not have to think about the moves; she was hardly even aware of her heart beating. Now for the flip around the highest bar, and the twirl...

She was elated. There it was again: that feeling that she was good at something. She felt that she could almost fly from the bars and float down, but she lowered herself as she had practiced and dismounted carefully. "Way to go!" Lauren said, throwing her arm around her friend's shoulders.

"Hey, when did you get so good?" Ryan said. "You looked just like a chimpanzee!"

Sarah took it as a compliment. She thanked her friends for their congratulations. They made her feel special. She was somebody in their eyes too, and she knew it.

She felt buoyed up by her success. It gave her the feeling that nothing could possibly go wrong that day. When Ms. Jefferson sprang a surprise math test, Sarah never for a moment thought that she wouldn't do well. Math was far from her best subject, but that afternoon the ideas she had been struggling with seemed to fall into place. Afterward, when papers were collected, murmurs of "Whew!" and "That was a hard one!" could be heard around the classroom. Alison tapped Sarah on the shoulder. "You looked like you were just zipping through it," Alison said with a touch of admiration. "Could you show me how you did number six?"

Sarah was happy to help her friend and even more pleased to have been asked. It was as though her moment on the playground had set off a chain reaction of positive feelings. Even when Shelton teased her about her hair, usually a sensitive subject for Sarah, she let it slide right off her.

She had to tell her parents, even if it spoiled her surprise. Her mother was away on a business trip, and her father came home early to cook supper. He listened attentively as she described move by move what she had done on the bars. "I'm proud of you," he said. He hugged her. "Look at those calluses," he said, opening her palms. "You must have worked hard."

"For more than a month," she said. "Can you and Mom come to the playground Saturday? I want you to see me do it!"

"You bet," her father said. "Now, how about helping me chop these vegetables?"

Later that evening, her mother phoned. Sarah could hear the smile in her voice when she asked her to tell her all the details of her day. "You're a very special person," *Sarah's parents respected and encouraged anything that was important to her.* her mother said. "There's nobody else like you in the entire universe."

"Oh, Mom," Sarah sighed. Her parents were always saying that. But it pleased her nonetheless. Maybe that's why they're fun to be with, Sarah told herself in a thoughtful moment. They let me be me. It was when some of her friends talked about their parents that she realized how lucky she was with hers. They were people she could talk to. They never said anything like "Why can't you be more like your sister?" as Anita's parents did, or made her feel that the things she liked were "dumb," as Jason complained that his did. They respected and encouraged anything that was important to Sarah—even the things that embarrassed her when she thought about them now, like the time she had tried to dig a hole to China, or that birthday when she had insisted on blue frosting for her cake. As far back as she could remember, Sarah had known that her mother and father would love her no matter what.

Not that they were pushovers. Uh-uh. Blue frosting was one thing; anything involving respect or responsibility was something else. If she neglected her homework, failed to follow through on a promise or acted without considering the needs and rights of others, Sarah was sure to hear of it. They were strict, but she always knew where she stood with them. Her parents had rules, and they expected them to be followed, but they never changed them in the middle of the game.

That's the thing about rules, Sarah thought as she walked her dog that evening. If you didn't have them, life would be confusing. Rules let you know when you've done something well, like play a game or clean your room or take

> **Feeling good about herself made her want to do things for other people.**

a math test. She remembered how she'd felt that afternoon after the test when Alison had asked her for help. It was funny how feeling good about herself made her want to do things for other people...and the other way around too. She wondered whether Lauren felt that way about showing her how to use the bars. Sarah smiled to herself as once again she reflected on her day and the way her parents had responded.

All week she continued to practice under Lauren's watchful eye. When Saturday morning came, it was all she could do to eat her breakfast. Butterflies seemed to have taken up all the available space in her stomach.

She could see the playground as the car came within sight of the schoolyard. It was almost empty. There were no children on the bars, no one waiting in line. Sarah stationed her parents in the best possible viewing place, wiped her hands on her T-shirt and stood for a moment looking at the bars and going through the routine in her mind. Then, without a glance at her parents, she shinnied up the pole and lunged forward.

It was a piece of cake. She heard her parents applaud when she reached the highest bar, heard them gasp when she executed her twirl.

It was a wonderful feeling! Sarah was a success—she had accomplished her goal. And the two people who meant most to her in all the world had been there to see her do it.

Once again: Sarah's story describes an everyday series of events. Yet it is such events that shape our lives. In the rest of this book, we'll take a closer look at these events and Sarah's feelings about them. We'll use them to illustrate ways in which you can help your children develop high self-esteem—ways that you can keep them "bound for success."

The Power of Self-Esteem

She enjoyed the feeling...a sense of *somebodiness*; a sense that she was worth something.

Everyone has his or her own way of defining self-esteem. For Sarah, it was "a sense of somebodiness."

For psychologist Nathaniel Branden, it was "the sum of self-confidence and self-respect. It reflects your implicit judgment of your ability to cope with the challenges of your life...and of your right to be happy...."

In the 1990 report of the California Task Force to Promote Self-Esteem and Personal and Social Responsibility, it was "Appreciating my own worth and importance and having the character to be accountable for myself and to act responsibly toward others."

However we define self-esteem, we can easily recognize those who have it. We have no trouble telling them apart from the merely conceited, who devote so much effort trying to impress us as "winners." Such people are typically trying to cover up a poor self-concept—a *lack* of self-esteem. Those with high esteem do not need to take center stage or to dominate. They may lead or follow as the situation suggests. They reach out to others, remain humble, and care deeply about people. They have no need to trumpet their successes. They are *successful*. They are a joy to be around. Their enthusiasm for life radiates like an aura.

Think of the truly successful people you know. Chances are, they display most or all of the following characteristics.

Characteristics of People with High Self-Esteem

Successful people have **direction**. They know where they are going. They establish priorities, set challenging goals and create realistic plans for achieving them.

Successful people are **positive**. They approach tasks with enthusiasm and persistence. When confronted with poor results, they address them as problem-solving opportunities, not as indications of failure. Instead of assigning blame for their setbacks, they do what is necessary to optimize the situation.

Successful people have **self-confidence**. They acknowledge their successes as a result of their capabilities. They are not afraid to take risks in pursuit of their goals or to accept any negative consequences of their decisions.

Successful people accept **responsibility**. They balance risk-taking with realistic self-assessment and do not back away from commitment. They are self-reliant but are comfortable calling on others for support.

Successful people are **communicators**, both actively and passively. They resolve conflict through assertiveness and understanding. They are effective listeners. They are able to persuade, yet they are open to other points of view.

Successful people are **caring**. Because success makes them feel good, they find ways to help others achieve success. They demonstrate appreciation for others and seek "win-win" situations.

Continued

Continued

Successful people have strong **spiritual values**. They may affirm their own being through traditional religious belief or through concern for the planet, appreciation of nature, or other such relationships with the universe outside themselves.

How Self-Esteem Keys Success

Such people, adults or children, are successful because their feeling of personal worth empowers them to set and achieve goals. Whether they measure success in money, creativity, fulfilling personal relationships, winning a spelling bee or mastering a routine on the playground bars, they have an awareness of what they can do coupled with a desire to do it.

Have you ever watched a group of youngsters hotdogging on their skateboards? I am always amazed at their skill and daring. It begins with a desire to do it and an awareness that they *can* do it. With such awareness, a child shrugs off scraped knees and peers' ridicule until he has mastered the basic skills. With

High self-esteem empowers people to set goals and achieve them.

practice comes increased confidence until he can do anything he wants on that skateboard. Such confidence, in turn, leads to the awareness that other accomplishments are within his power too.

A woman teaches her granddaughter to sew. The process begins with the child's admiration for her grandmother's handiwork—and her own belief that she can learn. Grandmother teaches her hand-stitching, assigning her small, simple projects. As she masters the skills, she takes on more complex work on the sewing machine. Eventually the confidence born of achievement leads her to design and make her own clothes—or to tackle another set of skills, such as those involved in tennis or computer programming.

Like Sarah, these children have allowed the skills they've learned to become an intrinsic part of the way they perceive themselves. Eventually this self-perception develops into an overall sense of competence. Instead of letting frustration or criticism send them into a downward spiral of discouragement and self-doubt, this sense leads them to seek new and creative paths to attainment of their goals. Such achievement in turn gives them the self-confidence to take the risks necessary to acquire new skills. In contrast, the child with a negative self-concept gives in too readily to discouragement. Typically he or she lacks the desire or confidence to set positive goals. Such pronouncements as "Skateboarding's boring," or "Sewing? That's for nerds" are very often covers for "I can't," "I'm not good enough," or "I don't deserve to." If Sarah had been a child with poor self-esteem, she might have given up the first time she fell off the bars. She might have taken Lauren's advice as negative criticism instead of positive encouragement. Chances are she would never have decided to perfect her routine in the first place.

And what guided Sarah—what guides any child—down the path to high self-esteem? Psychologists and child-development experts are nearly unanimous in identifying two factors:

- The child's **sense of personal value**: "I am important to myself and to other people. I am lovable."

- The child's **sense of competence**: "I can do things that people respect. I have something to offer to the world."

Succeeding chapters will show you how you can help develop such feelings in your children. Before you go on, fill in this questionnaire to assess how you're doing so far.

Are You Helping Your Children Develop Their Sense of Personal Worth?

On the line to the left of each statement, use a number from 1 through 5 (1 = poor; 5 = excellent) to indicate how you rank yourself.

___ I can identify several strengths I have.

___ I welcome challenges in my life.

___ I am motivated to accomplish things for myself without encouragement or praise.

___ I have personal goals that I am actively trying to achieve.

___ I take responsibility for my own actions.

___ I help my child set reasonable goals.

___ I share my vision for the future with my child.

___ I watch out for my child's positive behavior and give praise for it.

___ I let my child know I feel good about myself and that I can learn from my mistakes.

___ I pay special attention to finding and developing my child's uniqueness.

___ I take time to listen to my child and talk with her about her interests and activities.

___ I give my child responsibility so he will feel useful.

___ I encourage my child to help others and to respect diversity of values, backgrounds and norms.

___ I regularly discuss my values with my child, explaining the reasons for my decisions and feelings.

Continued

Continued

__ I spend time with my child sharing favorite activities.

__ I show my child how much I care about her.

__ I use phrases that build self-esteem, such as "Thank you for helping," or "That was an excellent idea."

Now total your score.

- If you scored 70 or above, congratulations! Your children should be well on the road to exemplary self-esteem.

- If you scored from 60 to 70, you're doing something right. Chances are your children have good self-esteem.

- If you scored from 40 to 59, most likely your children's self-esteem could use a boost. As you read on, compare what you're doing with the tips and techniques suggested in this book.

- If you scored below 40, your children may well have negative self-esteem. Fortunately, this need not be a permanent condition. Raising your children's self-esteem is simply a matter of changing habits—yours and theirs.

And if your perception of your children's self-esteem doesn't seem to match your score? It may be necessary for you to reassess your answers. As you read on, think about your parenting techniques and consider how you might start doing things differently.

After all, what's more important than your children's success?

Your Unconditional Love: The First Key to Self-Esteem

As far back as she could re-member, Sarah had known that her mother and father would love her no matter what.

"Children value themselves to the degree that they have been valued," Dorothy Corkille Briggs teaches us. The foundation for Sarah's self-esteem was the extent to which her parents' love made her feel worthy. Before she could develop a feeling of competence, she first had to know that she "belonged." She had to know that her parents would never hold back their love as a condition of her actions; that they valued her for the person she was. *For a child to have a healthy, positive self-image, it is critical for her to know without a doubt that she is a worthy and significant person in her parents' eyes—that they love her unconditionally.*

Unconditional love. We've heard the phrase so often it's become almost meaningless. Very likely you're thinking, "What's he saying—if I get on my son's case about his messy room, that means I don't find him worthy or significant? If I tell my daughter she'd get better grades if she weren't so lazy, it means I don't *love* her? What about limits? What about discipline?"

All good questions. Now let me ask you one: while setting limits and disciplining your children, are you conscientious in letting them *know* you love them?

Think about the words you use. Do you say, "You know, your messy room really bothers me"? Or do you say, "Clean up this pigsty! Were you born in a barn?"

Do you say, "You've always done well in English. Is there some reason you're having trouble now?" Or do you say, "You're not stupid—you're just lazy! No TV for you!"?

"Be careful what you say to your children," Nathaniel Branden wrote in *Honoring the Self.* "They may agree with you. Before calling a child 'stupid' or 'clumsy' or 'bad' or 'a disappointment,'...consider the question, 'Is this how I wish my child to experience himself or herself?'"

Words Have Power

What we say to and about our children are their earliest indications of their value as human beings. Our words are mirrors in which a child sees

> **Our words are mirrors in which a child sees himself reflected.**

himself reflected. All too often, those reflections diminish a child's sense of self. According to motivational speaker Zig Ziglar, of every one hundred reinforcers heard in the typical home, only five are positive. As for "negative reinforcers," they sound something like this:

"What are we going to *do* with you?"

"We don't expect too much of her; she does what she can."

"You're so shy! Don't you ever have anything to say?"

"You don't care about anyone but your own selfish self!"

"*You* take him; I've had to put up with him all day!"

"You idiot!"

Not pretty, are they? Most of us adults would feel beaten down if we heard phrases like these directed at us. Think of how a child must feel when her "self-portrait" is largely made up of such phrases.

Negative reinforcers, however, are not always so obvious. Often they are conveyed through indifference or insensitivity, from which the child may rightly infer judgment, criticism or comparison. How might Sarah's story have been different had her father responded to her account of her day with a plainly disinterested "That's nice"? Or if her parents, however gently, had invalidated what was important to her: "But don't you think chocolate frosting would be much nicer than blue?"

You may indeed love your child un-conditionally. But will he know it if so many of his "reflections" are negative? Any notion repeatedly reinforced becomes a habit. A child hears "you're selfish (lazy, stupid, bad)" often enough, or infers "I'm unimportant (uninteresting, slow, foolish, bad)" often enough, and she comes to regard it as true.

> *Negative reinforcers help to form a child's negative feelings about himself.*

Such a child may never develop high self-esteem. He may grow up convinced of his inadequacy and settle for a marginal life. He may build defenses by bragging, bullying or showing off. Or he may withdraw into fantasies and loneliness to cover up the feeling that nothing he can do in the real world will amount to anything.

Twenty-One Hugs a Day

By age four, most children have a well-developed self-image, whether positive or negative, based on reflections from their parents. Negative self-esteem is a *learned habit*, and, fortunately, like any negative habit it can be broken. But to break it requires constant positive attention by you, the parent. *The most important thing we can do for our children's self-esteem is to let them <u>know</u> they're loved unconditionally.*

A friend once said to me, "Everyone needs 21 hugs a day—seven for subsistence, seven for maintenance, and seven for growth." Of course, these are in addition

> *"Subsistence hugs" convey that home is a safe place to be.*

to actual, physical hugs. "Subsistence hugs" are the basic necessities of life—food and shelter, yes, but also the sense that home is a safe haven, a place they can depend on. Even a child growing up in poverty can have high self-esteem if she knows that home is a place where she can count on finding emotional sustenance.

"Maintenance hugs" come from connection to a family. A child needs

> **"Maintenance hugs" demonstrate parents' unconditional love.**

to be in a caring, nurturing environment and feel secure in her parents' love in any circumstances—even when they are expressing disapproval or anger.

Anna was a single mother who worked evenings. It was the responsibility of her daughter, Brooke, to wash and put away the dishes. But often as not Anna came home to find a sink piled high with dirty dishes and her daughter horizontal in front of the TV set. One evening after Anna had had a particularly frustrating day, she and her daughter got into an intense argument. As Brooke stormed off to her room, her mother called after her, "I *hate* you when you act this way!"

At once Anna realized what she had said. She followed Brooke to her room. "I'm sorry," she said. "That's not what I meant. I don't like what you did, but it doesn't mean that I don't like *you*." By giving Brooke a "maintenance hug," Anna showed that she cared about Brooke though she was angry at her daughter's actions.

> **"Growth hugs" build pride.**

As for "growth hugs," these are the self-esteem builders that develop a child's sense of pride. Any time you praise your child for a job well done, you're giving him a growth hug, so look for opportunities to do so.

Jackson played Little League baseball. He loved the game, but he was not an exceptional athlete. So far this season, he had been at bat 15 times without a hit. On this day, his father and older brother were in the stands. Jackson practiced with them whenever he had the chance, and he hoped that this was the day he would get his first hit.

Sure enough—his first time up, Jackson hit the ball squarely. He saw it heading for the outfield, and he knew he had a hit. He was so excited that he rounded first base with his head down— and was tagged out at second.

After the game, Jackson's father and brother did not mention his base-running mistake. They congratulated him on his successful hit. They were proud of him, and they told him so. Jackson went home with a big smile on his face. His family's "growth hug" gave Jackson pride in his accomplishment.

Or, in the words of a song one of my children once brought home from school:

I hate to hear what I'm doing wrong
Every day of the year;
I'd rather hear what I'm doing right
And where do I go from here?

It's impossible for your child to know you find him worthy of love if your feelings aren't reflected by your words and actions. On the next page are some guidelines to follow to let him know he's "doing something right"— that in your estimation he's a special person who can achieve anything he aims for.

Tips for Demonstrating that You Have
Confidence in Your Child

1. **Listen to how you talk to your child.** For a week, make a mental note to pay attention to what you say and the tone in which you say it. Consider how you would feel if someone talked that way to you. Consider how *you're* feeling when you say it. Then find a corrective, positive way to state what you're feeling: not with a snarl but with a smile; not "Can't you do anything right?" but "Here, would you like me to show you an easier way to do it?" This is a skill that needs to be developed and practiced, but the results will be invaluable to your children.

2. **Never tie your love to your child's actions.** Love your child without conditions because of who she is, not what she does. Make sure that discipline and correction are accompanied by sincere expressions of love. Let her know that it's *because* you love her that you are showing her more appropriate ways to behave. Let her think you're unfair, totally out of touch, even stark-raving mad, but don't let her question your love.

3. **Be negative toward the behavior, positive toward the child.** Always be sure when disciplining your child that it's his *behavior* you disapprove of, not him—not "Bad boy!" but "It really bothers me when you hit your sister. What's the problem?" Not "You're a liar!" but "I can't trust what you say when it doesn't match the facts."

4. **Find the good and applaud.** In *The One-Minute Manager*, Kenneth Blanchard and Spencer Johnson advise business

Continued

Continued

executives to "catch people in the act of doing something right." That goes triple for parents. Be on the lookout for your child's successes, even the small ones, and praise her, praise her, praise her! Show that you find her worthy and capable by giving her appropriate responsibilities.

5. **Set specific limits.** Make sure your child knows in advance your expectations or rules and the consequences for not living up to them: "You cannot watch TV on school nights until your homework is done and checked by me." Don't make the rules a one-sided arrangement. Allow the child input on what he thinks is fair, but make sure that you, the parent, have the final say. Explain why the rules are in his best interest and be sure to give praise when he observes them.

6. **Take the initiative in resolving conflict.** Never carry a grudge against your child for misbehaving. Don't continue to criticize her for inappropriate behavior after you've already addressed it. Teach her how to avoid carrying around self-defeating resentments by taking the lead in making up after an argument.

Building a Sense of Competence

She was elated. There it was again: that feeling that she was good at something.

"Nothing succeeds like success." Like many old sayings, this one carries a great deal of truth. It is through achievement that we develop the inner feeling of competence that leads to self-esteem.

It's a feeling we can almost *hear*. It's the voice of a child saying with determination, "I can do it myself." It's the voice inside us that says, "I can (tie my shoes, ride a bike, begin a new job). I can do things I am proud of and for which people respect me." By the time Sarah set out to master the bars, she knew this feeling well. The knowledge that she *had* succeeded in the past gave her the confidence to strive for *new* successes.

Success is the greatest motivator of success. A man takes up running because his doctor advises him to exercise. At first it's all he can do to huff and puff for a quarter mile. But each small success becomes an inducement to greater success. Before long he's checking the electronic timer as he crosses the finish line of another ten-kilometer race, elated that he's lopped a second off his personal best. Next year, maybe he'll try a marathon.

> **Success is the greatest motivator of success.**

As a parent you've observed this concept in action. A baby learns first to sit up, then to stand while you support him, then to take tentative steps while holding on to your hands, then to pull himself to a standing position. By this time he's nearly ready to walk. All he needs is the self-confidence necessary to risk letting go and take those first steps on his own.

And where does he get that confidence? One source is his *previous successes*—he's already mastered sitting, standing and "cruising." The other source is *you*. Remember the praise you lavished on your baby when he accomplished each stage of this learning process? Your encouragement, coupled with his desire to walk, led him to that first tremendous feeling of success.

If your child doesn't seem to have had that feeling for a while, there are two questions you should be asking yourself:

1) "What are his areas of competence?" and

2) "What have I done to encourage him *lately*?"

Our responsibility as parents is to discover what our children like to do and to guide them in doing it well. Our own daughter Kristina was singing as soon as she could talk. It was something she liked to do. My wife would sing with her at all hours of the day. When she was eight, we enrolled her in a children's theater program. Her first experience singing before an audience was as a rabbit in *Charlotte's Web*. Soon afterward, she began taking voice lessons. Her mother supervised her practice sessions whenever possible to help maximize her progress. We provided further encouragement by taking her to professional concerts and musical theater. Meanwhile, Kristina continued to participate in school and community musical events. Last summer, at age ten, she performed before an audience of 26,000 people—singing "The Star-Spangled Banner" at a major-league baseball game. Kristina knows she's a singer—we tell her so, her audiences tell her so, and most importantly she tells herself so.

> *Our responsibility as parents is to discover what our children like to do and to guide them in doing it well.*

It's crucial that your children's achievements be in areas that are important to them. *Don't* trap them into pursuing goals that are not their own, and don't try to assume ownership of their achievements. It's only by achieving our own goals that we attain the sense of mastery, the sense of *control over our own lives* that builds self-esteem. I know of a former major-league pitcher, one whose name any fan would recognize, who claims never to have felt successful as a ballplayer, not even when he pitched in the World Series or was selected to the All-Star team. Baseball was not something he chose; it was something his father wanted for him. Today, as the owner of a small business, he has found the personal fulfillment in his achievements that he never knew in baseball. He has taken control of his life.

If children make decisions based on their personal goals and feel positive about what they are doing, they *will* feel that they have a certain degree of control over their lives. And that feeling can't help but lead to greater confidence, self-esteem, and subsequent successes.

How Do You Guide Your Children Toward Achievement?

Younger children may develop pride in achievement through acquiring simple skills we parents can easily teach.

Ian was full of tears on his first morning at kindergarten. He was literally behind the other children even before he entered the classroom because he didn't know how to climb stairs. His family lived in a one-story house, and now Ian's mother realized that they rarely visited homes with stairs. That afternoon she took him downtown to the courthouse with its long stone staircase. By the end of the day he had mastered the art of climbing stairs. He went back for his second day of school full of pride in his success. By teaching him a new skill, his mother had helped him *put himself in control* of his new situation.

A success as simple as Ian's can point a child down the path to future successes. It can work with older children too.

❧

Connor and Eve planned to set up a lemonade stand in a park across the street from their apartment. They were ready to spend their allowance money on supplies, but they didn't know a thing about making lemonade, let alone running a business. When their father heard them making plans, he offered to help them list the things they would need and guided them in what to charge if they wanted to make money. *He* gave the guidance—and the praise when they counted up their profits at the end of the week—but *they* made the decisions, did the work and spent the earnings. The success was all theirs.

❧

These of course are simple examples. Encouraging your child's achievements often requires a greater commitment. But as Benjamin Bloom wrote in *Developing Talent in Young People,* "Given the right conditions, almost any child can rise higher, live better, shine more brightly. There is a talent hiding in almost every child, and parents can help nurture it into full flower."

> *"There is a talent hiding in almost every child, and parents can help nurture it into full flower."*

The first requirement of this nurturing process is that we be good observers. Watch your children at play and at a variety of activities. Be aware of what they like to do, what excites them, what their dreams and aspirations are. Then help them convert these desires into achievement by providing the opportunity to pursue them. Give your child a sketch pad or a set of Lego blocks; enroll him in a swimming class or a soccer program; allocate a part of the back yard or a window box for a garden. Suggest siblings, relatives, or family friends who might help advance him a step or two in his area of enjoyment.

To encourage your child to develop a variety of interests, fill his environment with interest-sparkers. At home these may include books, magazines, newspapers, games, hobbies, even video. In the community they may include visits to libraries, museums, and athletic and cultural events. Talk about different ways that people earn a living and spend their leisure time. Expose your child to as many opportunities as your time and resources allow—and then make extra time and find additional resources. Watch out for hints of interest or aptitude and follow up on them. What's required of you will depend on your own child's passions, but it's crucial for you to *get involved.*

One example: A four-year-old tapping out a rhythm on a chair may be showing an interest in music. Get her a toy instrument and see what develops. If she shows continued enthusiasm, she may be ready for lessons. If private instruction is not a reality due to budget constraints, check into classes at community recreation centers. You'll need to put time, care and effort into the process, but it will pay off as your child develops self-confidence.

These suggestions will help set your children on the path toward achievement. To keep them on that path when frustration and discouragement arise will require additional help from you. We'll look into that in the next chapter. Here are a few more tips for guiding your children toward those first successes.

Tips for Making the Most of Your Child's Achievements

1. **Give children control.** Point them toward achievement and the feeling of power by allowing them to make age-appropriate decisions. A three-year-old may decide what clothes he wants to wear—even if they don't match. A six-year-old can choose the route for a special parent-child walk. An eight-year-old can go shopping with you and choose a birthday gift for his grandmother. Give all children turns to choose the activities on special "family nights" or weekend outings.

Continued

Continued

(They may have to be reminded in advance to thank their siblings for choosing such a "fun activity," even if it may be boring to *them*.)

2. **Encourage responsibility.** Take time to teach your children age-appropriate tasks to do around the house: sweeping, feeding the dog, watering plants, etc. Teach them other age-appropriate jobs also, such as making a phone call, programming the VCR or baking a pie. Knowing how to do something on their own will build confidence and a sense of control.

3. **Model the behavior you want to see in your children.** Talk to them about your own special interests and achievements—the ones that give you esteem now and those that gave you esteem as a child. Let them see your enthusiasm and be aware of your pride in your achievements.

4. **Don't neglect praise.** Applaud your child for every small achievement. Hang his paintings on your kitchen wall. Better yet, hang them in your workplace and make sure he sees them when he visits. Attend every piano recital and award ceremony. Devise your own system of rewards for household tasks well done. After a time internal motivation will take over and success will become its own reward, but even then your praise will contribute to your child's self-esteem.

5. **Remember that success comes at many levels.** Your children don't need to be gold-medal winners in order to gain esteem from their achievements. "Victory" for some is to finish the race, not to come in first or second or even in the top one hundred. Let your children find their own level of success—even if it may not match your expectations.

Goal Setting: Drawing a Map for Achievement

...**h**aving a particular goal and
a plan for reaching it seemed to focus her efforts.

Consider two children; let's call them Pat and Robin. On New Year's morning Pat makes these resolutions: I will get better grades; I will earn more spending money; I will take up a new hobby. Robin writes down these resolutions: I will earn A's in math and history next semester; I will be mowing five lawns each week by July 1; I will learn woodworking and make a toy chest as a present for my sister by her birthday, October 22.

Now, who do you think is more likely to have kept his or her resolutions by year's end? If you said "Robin," give yourself a gold star. Pat had a "wish list." Robin *set goals.*

Most people are aware of the importance of goals, but many of us tend to confuse them with good intentions. Psychologist Bobbe Sommer, an authority on goal setting, likens a goal to a *set point*: a central tendency, like a setting on a thermostat, toward which we adjust. If we have no clear goals, our set point is zero. "If you don't know what you want, you're guaranteed not to get it," Sommer advises. It's no wonder we get discouraged over New Year's resolutions. If Sarah had not planned to perfect a specific set of skills by a specific date, she might have had a lot of fun on the bars, but she wouldn't have known the esteem that comes from achievement. Without goals, there *is* no achievement. It's like trying to find your way without a destination.

But when we set goals, we examine what is important to us and focus our energy on it. We have a clear and specific outcome in mind and a strategy for getting there. We have not only a destination but a map—one we have drawn ourselves.

Think back to an outstanding success of your own, a time when you achieved something that completely satisfied you. Chances are your goal was specific. Chances are you devised a clear plan for achieving it. And chances are that early in the process you took the trouble to *write down your goal*.

Keeping goals in our head does not produce the same results as writing them down. Written goals are reminders to ourselves to be accountable, invested and committed. In *Five Steps to Success*, Leo Hauser cites a Harvard Business School study that took a random sampling of 100 graduating seniors. All had verbally expressed their aspirations of success (i.e., to get rich), but only ten of them had actually written down their specific goals. Ten years later, those ten students owned 96 percent of the total wealth of the original 100-student sample.

> **Written goals are reminders to be accountable, invested and committed.**

Are you a list maker? Do you take a written list with you when you go grocery shopping? Do you write down daily or weekly "to-do" lists? Those lists are short-term goals. Don't you find that when you make a list you tend to come home with what you actually need, as opposed to when you simply pull items off the shelves? Don't you feel a greater sense of satisfaction when you cross items off a list than when you simply scurry around trying to get things done? Doesn't it make you feel successful? That's how goals help us move forward. They give us a sense of purpose; and when accomplished, they make us feel capable.

Unfortunately, apart from such lists few of us bother to write down our goals. This is one reason why our children don't set goals—we fail to model the behavior for them. But your children will best realize the achievement that builds self-esteem by setting goals—whether the goal is to earn money for a stereo system, have a poem printed in the school newspaper, earn a spot on the soccer team, make a new friend, or perfect a routine on the playground bars. As Bobbe Sommer puts it, "It doesn't matter what your goal is; it only matters that you *know* what it is."

Turning Your Children Into Goal Setters

It is never too early to start teaching your children about goals. We do it all the time, usually with a promised reward to motivate them to complete a task: "Now, how about getting your toys put away? If you do it by eight o'clock, we'll read a special story at bedtime." "Let's all

> *Guide your children to self-generated tasks with achievement as its own reward.*

pitch in and get the leaves raked up, and we'll go to the zoo." Such tangible rewards do help make children achievement oriented, particularly when they are very young. The next step is to get them to move from parent-imposed tasks with a reward as inducement to self-generated tasks with achievement as its own reward—in other words, to goal setting.

Start with a *family* goal. Make it something the children ask for, e.g., a special vacation trip. (A major project such as planning a vacation serves to illustrate clearly the procedures you'll follow and the steps you'll take; in actuality, you'll probably want to start out with something less grand, such as cleaning out the garage or training a puppy.) Involve the whole family in allocating the money and other necessary preparations for the trip. Dad and Mom will pitch in from their salaries, and the children will contribute an appropriate share from part-time jobs (if old enough) or from chores around the house. Sit down together and let the family negotiate contributions for all tasks (including non-monetary tasks such as obtaining maps) with dates by which they are to be done. Write the goal on a sheet of paper: "The Alvarez family is spending the third week of July at Yellowstone National Park." Then write a few intermediate goals that are steps toward achieving this goal. Specify everybody's task—"Alex and Kim will contribute $50 toward costs by painting the backyard fence by Saturday May 20." Have the family discuss and agree on these specifications. Decide on a series of rewards for completion of intermediate goals. If possible, have them relate in some way to the main goal. If it's a camping vacation at Yellowstone Park, Alex and Kim can pick out a new tent as a reward for painting the fence. For a shorter-term goal, such as cleaning out the garage, an intermediate reward can be pizza once the magazines are sorted and bundled. Always reward any task completed with a verbal pat on the back: "Alex and Kim—great job painting the fence. I couldn't have done it better myself!"

After you've accomplished your family goal, help each child set a simple age-appropriate personal goal of his or her own—doing an extra-credit book report, mastering a new computer game, taking a challenging bike ride. Guide the child in setting a realistic yet timely date for completion. Where there are no built-in criteria for achievement (e.g., the destination for the bike ride), have him suggest one (e.g., an "A" on the book report; a score in the game that to him constitutes "mastery"). Post his goal on the refrigerator. When he's achieved it, stamp it with a colorful sticker to indicate a job well done. Be sure also to offer *specific* verbal praise that addresses his efforts, attitude and feelings: "You biked to Elgin and back? That's 35 miles! I guess all that training and planning was worth it. You must feel as proud as if you'd won an Olympic gold medal!"

> *Guide your child in setting and achieving his own goals.*

Now your child is on a winning streak. It's time for her to decide some of her own short-term and long-term goals. These of course are highly personal choices, but give her the guidance she needs to make them meaningful and to help her set up a plan for achieving them:

Parent: "What would you like to do by the end of summer that would really make you feel like you accomplished something?"

Child: "I think I'd like to earn some money for school clothes."

Parent: "How much do you think would be enough?"

Child: "A hundred dollars would be nice. I could buy a couple of special outfits, shoes and all!"

You could then discuss how she could earn the money, suggesting age-appropriate ways to do it. Let her take the lead, but help her calculate how much she could possibly earn from each type of job. Then guide her in setting up an action plan and putting it into written form. This plan should start with the final goal and a date for achieving it. It should specify the steps she will take toward achievement (e.g., making a list of her applicable skills, talking to friends who might have advice, allocating time to look for jobs, obtaining any special equipment she will need) with self-generated deadlines for each. Help her identify a few intermediate goals along the way. Have her design her own series of rewards to give herself as she accomplishes each intermediate goal—going to the movies after securing the jobs, for example, or a weekend with no jobs after she earns her first $50. A wall calendar or day-by-day chart makes an outstanding organizer for goal setting. Your child can gain a sense of achievement by planning and then marking off steps taken toward her goal and intermediate goals attained along the way.

Set up a written plan that specifies the steps your child will take towards achieving her goal.

Your child's goals must be age-appropriate. Your twelve-year-old might want to earn $100, while your six-year-old might want to learn to roller skate. What is short term to a twelve-year-old might be long term to a six-year-old. You need to be the judge of your own child's maturity. Younger children would do best to choose only short-term goals, while teenagers might select goals that take even a year or two to complete.

Examples of Appropriate Goals
for Your Children

Short-term goals (for children of various ages) include:

• planning a party for a few friends.

• learning a new song on the guitar.

• completing a week's homework without being reminded by parents.

• reading a book at a higher level of difficulty than one is used to.

Long-term goals include:

• raising one's math grade by the next report card.

• typing 60 words per minute.

• learning to play a new musical instrument.

• running a mile in under eight minutes.

• completing a science-fair project.

• selecting and applying to colleges.

Be sure that your child plans appropriate rewards for himself to mark milestones along the way.

Encourage your child to identify people who could help him achieve his goal—a friend who is a whiz at the computer game he's trying to master, a second cousin who's an admissions counselor at the state university. Suggest available resources that might help him in pursuit of the goal—libraries, classes, coaching, free government pamphlets. Have him add research and consultation time into his action plan. Help him to identify possible obstacles to achievement of his goal and to create an alternate plan for getting around them.

It is important to remember that goals change. They change for all of us—what might have been our most passionate desire five years ago may have been made irrelevant by changes in our lives or attitudes. How much more true is this of children, whose interests change faster than their shoe sizes! This is why it's important for younger children to limit themselves to goals they can achieve in a reasonable amount of time. If your child loses sight of her goal because her priorities change, *don't* let her become discouraged about goal setting. Guide her in channeling her efforts into a new goal appropriate to her maturity and interests.

It is also important to remember that goal setting always involves risk—not the sort of risk involved in sky diving or investing our life's savings in stock options, but the kind we face every time we leave what is comfortable and venture off into the unknown. To take any such risk involves courage and self-assurance, and this will come only after re-

> *Remember that it is the process and not just the end result that leads to healthy self-esteem.*

peated experiences with achievement and success. Until then, remember that it is the process and not just the end result that leads to healthy self-esteem. The pursuit of the goal and the rewards that mark milestones along the way will make it worth doing; the courage and self-assurance will surely follow.

Finally, it is important to remember that no one can set goals for anyone else. We all know parents who plan for their seven-year-old's admission to medical school, the National Football League, the Joffrey Ballet. We can set such goals for our children, and they may indeed achieve them, but they will only gain real satisfaction if they themselves want the goal as much as we want it for them. "But isn't it my role as a parent to help her decide what she wants to do?" you may ask. Yes—and the key word is *help*. That's all we as parents can do regarding our children's goals, if the desired outcome is their own self-esteem. We can help, but the choices must be their own. On the next page are a few more pointers to help your children make those choices.

Tips to Help Your Children
Set Beneficial Goals

1. **Model goal setting.** Discuss with your children your present goals and those you've accomplished in the past. Write down your own long- and short-term goals, your plans for achieving them, and the rewards you plan to give yourself along the way. Your children will be more inclined to set goals when they see you do it, and they'll have a blueprint to follow as well.

2. **Create goal portraits.** A great way for children to get involved in thinking about goals is by expressing their aspirations in art. By now you should be exposing them to all sorts of interest sparkers as suggested in the last chapter. Obtain a number of old magazines for them to browse through and have them cut out pictures of what they would like to accomplish and/ or have. These pictures are then pasted into a collage that becomes the "goal portrait."

3. **Schedule an annual goal-setting day.** Choose a date for everyone in the family to sit down together and plan goals for the year—family goals as well as personal goals. Discuss the direction of your lives: what you view as your needs and aspirations, individually and as a family. This is a time for each of you to reflect on what you want for yourselves, and how you want to share your strengths with others. Decide on some family goals for the coming year: vacations, home projects, getting through a week without turning on the TV. Limit your goals to a reasonably attainable number of long-

Continued

Continued

and short-term goals (in our family we have settled on five). At least one of them should be an other-directed goal, such as raising money for charity or tutoring a neighbor's child to help him raise his grades. Children's personal goals may be shared with the family or in some cases kept private. Then encourage them to write action plans for achieving each goal.

4. **Make contracts with your children.** Once your child has specified her goals and worked out a plan, help her put an official stamp on it with a written contract. Be clear on the steps she will take to achieve her main goal, the intermediate goals along the way, and the rewards she will earn (if any) at each stage. Solemnize the agreement with both your signatures. You'll find that such a "legal document" sharpens your child's focus and augments her chances of attaining her goal.

5. **Focus on one major goal at a time.** Your child will gain considerably more self-esteem by achieving one goal than by scrambling to make progress on five at once. On the other hand, if he sets many short-term goals that are intermediate steps to long-term goals, he can feel the satisfaction of success sooner and with greater frequency.

6. **Monitor progress.** Encourage your child to take at least one step each day, no matter how small, toward attainment of a goal. Have her mark her progress on her calendar. This will reassure her that she *is* making progress. Be lavish in handing out praise for each such small accomplishment.

Continued

Continued

7. **Discourage discouragement.** For some children, discouragement comes easily. Once your child has set goals and written an action plan, do everything you can to encourage him to follow through. This of course does not mean sneering at him for being a "quitter"—the idea is to *raise* his self-esteem, not tear it down! Start by suggesting some intermediate goals. If he has no problem completing daily assignments but experiences great anxiety with long-range projects, help him break the large projects into bite-sized pieces. The process may require more reinforcement from you at first, but pride in achievement will eventually become its own motivation. If a goal proves to be unrealistic, help your child reach a new agreement with himself. It's no disgrace to extend a date or to rechannel efforts into something more attainable. As long as he doesn't simply up and quit, he will realize success— and success can't help but build on success.

Visualization: Painting a Self-Portrait of Success

As she waited, Sarah went through the routine in detail in her mind.... "You can do it," she told herself silently.

Golf champion Tom Watson tells the story of the time he won the U.S. Open on the final hole by blasting out of a bunker so far below the green he couldn't even see the cup. The ball rose from the sand, hit the pin and dropped in. Years later, people still remark to Watson how lucky he was to have made the shot. But there was no luck involved. Tom Watson had practiced that shot in his mind 200 times, visualizing it going into the cup every time.

Athletes, business executives, musicians, world leaders—successful people of all kinds practice mentally by *visualizing* themselves as successful. They create an inner feeling of success by picturing their achievements in detail before they actually happen. Sarah knew "the thrill of victory" before she even mounted the bars—and because of it, she never doubted that she would succeed.

This is not a function of "willpower" but of imagination. Creative visualization works because of a basic psychological principle: your subconscious mind can't tell the difference between what is real and what you vividly imagine. It believes whatever your conscious, thinking mind tells it is so, and you feel and act in a way consistent with this belief.

If a child habitually visualizes herself as successful, she can approach the actual experience with the self-assurance consistent with success.

There's a catch here, however: In order for such "mental rehearsal" to work, a child must possess adequate self-esteem. Otherwise she sabotages herself with *negative self-talk*: "Who, me? I'm too—" dumb, fat, boring, lazy, weird, or some other false, destructive reflection. Such reflections send a message to her subconscious that success is impossible—that she doesn't *deserve* success. And her subconscious can't help but agree. Could Sarah have visualized her success if she'd had such thoughts as, "I'll never be as good as Lauren. I'm too clumsy. I think I'll just go home and watch TV"?

> *If a child habitually visualizes herself as successful, she can approach the actual experience with the self-assurance consistent with success.*

But remember: such negative self-assessments are nothing but habits, and habits can be broken. If your child combines visualization with *positive self-talk*—consciously telling himself that *he can do it*—he can in effect pull his self-esteem up by its bootstraps. These techniques work hand in hand to help him focus on a particular goal, and on the image of himself as a person with the power to choose, set, and achieve goals. "I *think* I can, I *think* I can" meets "I think, therefore I am."

Teaching Your Children to Visualize Success

Teaching children visualization and positive self-talk is easy. Convincing them it's going to work is the tough part. The first step is to do something about your own negative thought patterns—those you model as behavior for your child, and those you keep inside yourself.

It's a well-documented fact that our thoughts about ourselves tend to be negative—up to 85 percent of them, according to some studies. We focus on problems, not possibilities. We dwell on our setbacks and discount our successes. Instead of "I failed to get that promotion," we think "I'm a failure." Instead of "I made a mistake," it's "I'm a foul-up." We become so habituated to thinking that way that we can't imagine thinking any other way. Our attitudes toward goals become excuses for this negative self-perception: "I can't." "I don't have time." "What a dummy I am." "It's no use; I'm too (ugly, dull, uneducated); no good with (people, numbers, machines); the wrong (sex, color, age); tied down by my (kids, spouse, mother)."

Make a point of listening to your own self-talk over the course of a week. Tally the number of positive statements and negative statements. What sort of attitude are you transmitting to your children?

It is important for us as parents to "clean up our own act" before we start in on our children's. It is difficult to hand out praise if we don't feel praise-worthy ourselves or to transmit hope if we feel hopeless. Since self-perception is based on the way we habitually imagine ourselves, we must break the habit and replace it with one of viewing ourselves positively.

One way to start is with **personal affirmations**. Personal affirmations are positive statements about ourselves that are relevant to our life and the habits we want to change. Any time you find yourself indulging in negative self-talk, you replace

> *Positive self-talk can change the way we see ourselves.*

the statement with its opposite. Instead of "I didn't get that promotion— I'm a failure," try, "I was fully deserving of that promotion; next time I'll get it." In addition, write down a few positive self-statements that directly address your negative perceptions of yourself: "I am good at my job"; "I am a bright person, and my ideas are worthy of respect"; "I am a positive parent who encourages my children to succeed."

Make a point of *diligently repeating these affirmations aloud 21 times each day for 21 days.* There is of course nothing magic about the number 21. It's just an easy number to focus on, and many experts tell us that breaking any habit takes at least three weeks of consistent application.

As you're correcting your own negative self-talk, be alert to your children's. As a parent, you need to practice emphatic listening: Any time you hear your child say "I *hate* the way I look," "It's no use—I can't draw," "I'm too stupid to do fractions," correct her with a positive affirmation: "You mean you don't understand these problems. It doesn't mean you're stupid, it only means that fractions are tricky. Here, let's see if I can help you figure out how to do it." You need to correct your child's negative self-talk *every time you hear it*. You need to be as diligent about her emotional security as you are about her physical security.

Next, show her how to replace her negative self-talk with her own affirmations: "I like the way I look," "I'm learning to draw well," "I'm a bright kid, and I can handle fractions." Emphasize to your child that this is not being "phony." She's gotten into the habit of looking at herself in a negative way, and now she's replacing the habit with one

> *Show your child how to replace her negative self-talk with positive affirmations.*

that's more positive. Compare it with another negative habit she's broken through conscious effort, such as nail-biting. Suggest that she write down her affirmations on stickers or Post-Its™ and place them where she'll see them every day—on her dresser mirror, above her towel rack, on the inside cover of her school notebook. Remind her of the "rule of 21": to repeat her affirmations 21 times daily for 21 days.

Now comes the crucial step: positive self-talk can only work in combination with visualization. (There's a reason for this, having to do with the different functions of the left and right sides of the brain and how they work together.) Tell your child that during those three weeks you'd like him to spend 10 minutes every day picturing himself the way he would like to be—doing what he'd be doing, feeling what he'd be feeling if he had reached his most cherished goal, if he were the best possible "himself." Have him choose a quiet place where he can sit or lie comfortably, close his eyes, relax, and clear his mind of busy thoughts. Music may help him relax, but only if it's unobtrusive music. During his daily 10 minutes, he's to let nothing interfere with his visualiza-tion—not TV or the phone or worries about school. Let him hang a "Do Not Disturb" sign on his door if he wishes, and make sure that brothers and sisters respect his privacy. All he is to do during this time is to visualize himself in fulfillment of his goal.

It may take longer than three weeks, but if your child applies positive self-talk in combination with visualization, she will have placed herself firmly on the path to success. She'll find herself thinking and feeling like a success—perceiving herself as capable of setting goals and of following through to achievement.

To ease her way—and yours—here are a few more suggestions for gaining the most benefit from these techniques.

Tips for Guiding Your Child Toward a Positive Self-Image

1. **Banish "can't" and "try."** These two words encourage negative thinking and excuse-making. Urge your children to banish "I can't" from their thoughts when troublesome situations arise and replace it with "This is a challenge." You'll discover that such a change in a habit of attitude will lead to a change in a habit of action—their approach to problem-solving. Then declare war on "try"—as in "I'll try to get my homework done." *Try* gives us permission to fail. Consciously substitute "I'll work hard...," and see how attitudes and performance change.

2. **Surround yourself with positive people.** It's bad enough that we put ourselves down; too often we allow our so-called friends to do it to us. Encourage your children to seek friends who want them to succeed and avoid those who are jealous of other people's achievements or who ridicule their goals.

3. **Create a picture of success.** Children with low self-esteem may find it hard to get started with visualization. To give your child an idea of what he would be like if his goal were a reality, have him draw a picture of the way he would feel if he were the best possible person he could be. Children who lack confidence in their drawing ability can make it a verbal or written description.

Building a Positive Mental Attitude

She felt buoyed up by her success. It gave her the feeling that nothing could possibly go wrong that day.... It was as though her moment on the playground had set off a chain reaction of positive feelings.

I have a colleague who leaves this message on his answering machine: "Thank you for calling, and *create* a good day." What he means is to face the day with a positive mental attitude, to look on each moment as an opportunity to make our day and our world more positive. When we as parents do this we guide our children toward a positive attitude too—and that's a course that leads to success.

"Positive thinking" is not the same thing as high self-esteem. As we learned in the last chapter, the "I can't" feeling and its opposite, positive affirmation, are products of habit and imagination, not of will. But "a smile in our thinking" is a necessary prerequisite for high self-esteem. It creates a bottomless reservoir of positive feelings that help us overcome setbacks and self-doubt. Such feelings contribute to our success and to others' as well—as Sarah with her "chain reaction of positive feelings" could attest.

We all know about *negative* chain reactions—the old cliché of a falling row of dominoes. Encountering a negative person on your way to work can affect your whole day and that of everyone you come in contact with. Your negative encounters can lead you to snarl at your coworkers, your family, even the waiter who takes your lunch order.

A smile and a friendly face can have the opposite effect—and it goes far deeper than the difference between a good day and a bad one. Numerous studies have shown the relationship between a positive outlook and personal and professional success. Medical research indicates that our feelings can affect the prognosis of disease. Business experts emphasize the relationship between a manager's personal outlook and "the bottom line."

> *People with a positive attitude see themselves as having the power to make a difference.*

Psychologist Martin Seligman has made a detailed study of what he calls "explanatory styles"—people's tendency toward a positive or negative view of the world. Simply put, pessimists not only "see the cup as half empty instead of half full," they tend to regard the emptiness as permanent and beyond their control. Optimists, on the other hand, not only see the cup as half full, they look for ways to fill it to the brim. *They see themselves as having the power to make a difference.* But as the title of Seligman's book *Learned Optimism* implies, people with a negative outlook can *learn* to be positive— to get beyond the feeling that "nothing I can do could make a difference"; to become goal setters and achievers.

A Happy Face Can Lead to Happy Results

Building a positive attitude in your children is simply a matter of making it a habit—and once again, the way to encourage this habit is to model it yourself. "The only way to raise positive kids," writes Zig Ziglar in *Raising Positive Kids in a Negative World*, "is to start by becoming a positive parent." You can program yourself to "create a good day" for you and your children through enthusiasm, praise and a smile on your face.

Start by listening to the attitude you project when you talk to your children. Make a list of statements that indicate a negative attitude. Then write down a way you could say the same thing more positively. Change the attitude by changing the talk. Here are some examples.

Change Negative Talk into Positive Talk

Negative: "I've spent nine hours today slaving to put dinner on the table; the least you could do is help clean up!"

Positive: Let's all do our share, and we'll have time to play a game together after dinner."

Negative: "Can't you do *anything* right?"

Positive: "You made a mistake, but I'm proud of you for doing it yourself. It might work better next time if you'd..."

At first your children's attitude may be "Gee, Mom/Dad sure is acting *weird*." But if you're consistent, it's only a matter of time before your new attitude becomes "you"—and your children *recognize* it as you. Remember the 21-day rule, but *don't* expect to get up with a smile on your face every day for three weeks and find yourself transformed into a positive person on Day 22. This isn't magic, nor is it insincerity—it's *practice*.

> *With practice, positive actions will result in a genuinely positive attitude.*

You're turning a conscious (and self-conscious) act into a habit. If you start with positive *actions*, you'll end up with a genuinely positive *attitude*. It may take longer than 21 days, and you may feel uncomfortable while you're doing it, but think of the "positive chain reactions" you'll be starting.

❦

Al had a "learning moment" when he heard his eight-year-old son say to his four-year-old daughter, "That's the way it is in life; the big fish eat the little fish." It was something Al himself often said—and only now did he recognize how discouraging it was, how hopeless an attitude it conveyed.

At once Al set out consciously to change the energy in his home from negative to positive. He made a point of greeting everyone with a smile and a caring word. He watched for occasions to hand out verbal hugs that would make his children feel good about themselves: "I'm glad we're spending today together—just us. You two are so special to me." When he disciplined them, he made sure to address their behavior, not their feelings about themselves. He went out of his way to offer people help at home, at work, and on the street. At first he felt self-conscious: "What am I doing, trying to be a Boy Scout? This isn't me!" But within a month, he found that it had *become* him. More important, it was becoming the style in which his whole family related to one another. There were many fewer occasions on which Al felt it *necessary* to discipline his children—and many more incidents of laughter and sharing. His daughter was even complimenting the cat.

It's been my observation that a positive mental attitude leads children to develop a generosity of spirit: an attitude of caring, a habit of "random acts of kindness." When children feel good about themselves, they create room within themselves for concern about the welfare of others. They'll reach down and pick up a package someone has dropped while waiting in line at the post office. They'll help younger children from the neighborhood find the right school bus to board at the end of the day. They'll step to one side and give others room to pass on the sidewalk. They'll ask you to help them make cookies to welcome a new neighbor.

> *When children feel good about themselves, their concern for the welfare of others is heightened.*

In some instances, such a change in attitude may even point a child along his or her life's path.

⸙

Julie was a sullen fifteen-year-old with poor grades and no apparent goals beyond hanging out at the mall. When her parents suggested that she get involved in a community project—volunteering at a local nursing home—she made no effort to disguise her displeasure: "Who wants to be with a bunch of *old* people?" After her parents explained that the nursing home had a real need for someone to come in and occasionally play piano (Julie's one ongoing interest), she agreed grudgingly to try it.

At first Julie limited her interaction with the nursing-home residents to simply playing the piano for them. She found that their positive response to her music made her feel good about herself. This feeling kept her coming back, and it also began to create more positive feelings about other aspects of her life. After several months her growing positive feelings carried her beyond the level of "performance," and she let the nursing-home residents engage her in conversation. It was then that she began to discover how lonely and how *human* they were. She realized how much more it meant to them to have her talk and *listen* to them than simply to perform. She initiated a project of taking down their reminiscences and compiling them in a "memory book" for the home. By her senior year other volunteers had taken over the project, but by then Julie had become goal directed. She wasn't sure whether she wanted to be an advocate for the elderly or a geriatric nurse, but she knew that either choice meant college.

⸙

Modeling a positive mental attitude does not mean hiding your not-so-positive feelings. Once you've broken the "negativity habit," there will still be times when you feel less than terrific. Children need honesty from their parents. They need to see us experience the full range of human emotions—including sadness, anger, and other negative feelings. It gives them permission to support and love themselves when *they're* feeling negative. Even after you've made a positive attitude a habit, there will still be those bad days. Just don't miss a chance to initiate positive chain reactions when you can.

Tips for Helping Your Child
Create a Positive Attitude

1. **Defuse "negativity bombs."** Don't let a child's tantrum or sulk start a negative chain reaction. Do what it takes to keep him from going to bed unhappy or going off to school unhappy. This may mean a bedtime story, a quiet discussion or special preparation to smooth the next morning's routine. Let him know you care about him and about his feelings. Asking him to share his feelings can be wonderful therapy. And always follow up the discussion with a hug.

2. **Condition yourself to smile.** Your child will more readily develop a positive attitude the more she makes herself feel positive. Encourage her to surround herself with positive people, to read books that make her feel good, to laugh as often as she can. Even a "smiley face" on a mirror, trite as it may seem, can be an aid to positive feelings.

3. **Encourage positive behavior.** Get your children involved in projects that make them feel good, such as creative endeavors, reading uplifting books or helping other people. Talk to them about the small things they did each day to make themselves and other people feel good. Encourage them to

Continued

Continued

give of themselves to someone every day. Praise them for their acts of kindness. Urge them to think of themselves and to present themselves as positive—to hold their head high, smile and make eye contact when they greet people. Remind them that this is not being "phony"—it's *practice* for building a positive attitude. Suggest that they respond to "How are you?" with "Wonderful!" or "Just great!" They'll find themselves becoming more positive—and liking themselves for it.

Choosing Role Models

Sarah...hoped that she could someday be as good as Lauren, and she told her so.

At the end of one of my workshops for teachers several years ago, a young woman approached me and asked if my wife's name was Betty Jo. It turned out that when she was a high-school junior, my wife had been her art teacher. "She had been talking about offering a special class for advanced students," the woman told me, "and one day she stopped me in the hall and asked me if I was going to take it. Well, I hadn't even thought about taking it, because I'd never dreamed I was qualified. I was flattered that she thought I was. I ended up taking the class, and I loved it. When I think about why I became a teacher, I remember that incident and how Mrs. Simmons made a difference in my life. Could you tell her 'Thank you' for me?"

I couldn't wait to get home and tell my wife—and was amazed when she couldn't recall this student. This taught me an important lesson: we don't always know whose role models we are. As the years go by, Lauren may not remember Sarah, but it's a cinch that Sarah will remember Lauren, her model for excellence on the bars.

A *role model* can be anyone we admire and seek to emulate. I can remember three in particular who enriched my life. The first was a sister five years older than I. She was a fine student and a model for achievement in school. She would sit at the table with me when I did my homework, and I remember how her caring helped me feel special.

Then there was my first-grade teacher, Mrs. Fiefield. She taught me reading and writing, the fundamentals of baseball, and the recognition that I was worth something. In the eyes of a six-year-old boy, she was larger than life. Years later, when I was an education major at Southern Oregon State College, there was Mrs. Fiefield! She had returned to college for advanced training. One of the greatest thrills of my life was to walk down the aisle with her to receive our diplomas together.

My third role model was someone I knew only briefly. When I was twelve, I had a weekend job caddying at a local golf course, and one Saturday I went 18 holes with a man who was visiting from another town. He showed a genuine interest in me, in what I liked to do and what I thought. I never forgot how caring he was, and I try always to remember that feeling when dealing with others.

Our role models may be many and varied: the older child who has a skill we admire and is generous in sharing its secrets; the neighbor, relative or scout leader who instills in us a lifelong love of photography, cooking or woodcraft; the teacher, coach or mentor who inspires us to excellence; the friend whose friendship propels us to do our best. These are all *positive role models*.

But children may also choose *negative role models*, and this choice is often a function of self-esteem. A person who feels unvalued may seek "respect" in the form of fear and envy; a person who sees no hope of success through achievement may resent the achievements of others. Such a child may choose to emulate the adult who settles disagreements with violence, the older child who flaunts authority or who gains what she wants by manipulating others, the authority figure who uses his power to oppress others.

> *Parents need to guide their children in choosing positive role models.*

It is we parents who are our children's first role models. It is we whose guidance will influence their choice of others. It's up to us to be sure that our children reject negative role models and choose positive ones—starting with ourselves.

Steering Your Children Toward Positive Role Models

"Parents are not only the ultimate teachers; they are also the models, for our children learn by imitating our ways,"

> *"...our children learn by imitating our ways."*

wrote Beverly Neuer Feldman in *Kids Who Succeed*. "Teachers, relatives and friends can be influential in helping give our children direction, but parents build the character that lasts."

Child-development experts recognize three phases in children's learning. In their earliest years children learn chiefly through *instruction*. This is the "how-to" time of life, the time when our influence is strongest. We teach our children how to brush their teeth, how to cross the street safely, how to say "please" and "thank you," how to share, how to recite their ABCs. We're their first and most important instructors in the physical, social, moral, emotional and intellectual realms—in *everything*.

Awesome, isn't it? Your child goes off to kindergarten thinking that everything you've taught him is the way things are supposed to be, so you must be very careful and very thorough about what you teach him. You must repeat each lesson until the desired behavior becomes a habit, reinforce appropriate behavior with praise and address inappropriate behavior whenever it is displayed. If you are diligent in your positive instruction in these early years, you'll go a long way toward "immunizing" your child against the negative modeling of other adults and peers.

❦

Six-year-old Brent went to a friend's birthday party at a pizza restaurant. That evening, his parents received a call from the birthday boy's mother. "I want to thank you for the present Brent gave Dan," she said, "but I want to thank you especially for the way he behaved. Some of the other kids were yelling and running around the tables, but Brent just sat there eating his lunch and talking to Dan. I just want to let you know that he's welcome at our house any time."

Brent's parents had spoken to him often about the right way to behave in restaurants, stores and movie theaters. Here was their first indication of his behavior in such situations outside their supervision. "Brent, I'm proud of you," his father told him. "Your mom and I are really glad that you know how to behave in public places—even when your friends are misbehaving."

⁕

Around age nine, the second phase begins. Emphasis shifts from learning by instruction to learning through imitation. This is the time of *modeling*, when parents find that "Do as I say, not as I do" won't work. If we want children to be unselfish, we must model unselfishness. If we don't want them to swear, we must watch our own language. We are being observed very closely—and so are their teachers, their peers, and others in the community. They are understudies waiting to go on stage and play our roles.

Don't sell your child's perception short. He can spot insincerity a mile away. If we model dishonesty, aggressiveness, a cynical attitude toward the law or disrespect for others, *he will emulate us*—regardless of what we happen to <u>say</u> about such behavior. He may display our "as I say" attitudes in our presence, but he will copy our "as I do" behavior when out of our sight.

It's a simple equation. We *are* role models to our children, whether or not we choose to be. They may or may not admire us, but they will mirror us. Being a positive role model means being careful to model the behavior we want them to mirror.

> *After ourselves, our children's most significant role models are their teachers.*

After ourselves, our children's most significant role models are their teachers. An inspiring teacher can influence a child for life. Unfortunately, so can an uncaring, slovenly or inept one. The teacher who plainly hates her job, displays a cynical attitude toward life or diminishes her students' esteem with sarcasm can be a role model every bit as much as the upbeat, caring teacher who encourages learning and takes a personal interest in her students' success.

How can you tell whether your child's teacher is a positive role model? One thing you can do is volunteer to help out in the classroom. You can observe the teacher in action and note the positive and negative qualities he presents. (Even a person you perceive as a negative role model will have some good qualities.) Then you talk with your child. Point out the teacher's positive qualities: "He's really helpful when someone is having trouble understanding something." Guide your child in identifying and expressing his or her feelings about

Help your child to look for her teacher's positive qualities.

the teacher's negative qualities: "Does it bother you that Mr. Handler sometimes seems impatient with the kids in your class?" Ideally, you can establish a relationship with the teacher, make sure he understands your goals for your child and help him to focus on those goals.

In the real world, of course, such a procedure is often impractical. Working parents don't necessarily have time to volunteer in the classroom, and the typical teacher has many children's goals to consider—not to mention the principal's, the PTAs, the teachers' union's and the school board's. In a less-than-ideal situation, the teacher might well regard an attempt to get her to focus on your particular agenda as unwarranted interference. But there is still a way to guide your child in emulating her teachers' positive qualities while rejecting the negative: by *talking to your child*. Encourage her to talk about teachers she has liked and disliked and why she feels that way about them: "How did Ms. Brenner inspire you to do more than you thought you were capable of?" "What is it about Ms. Driscoll that makes you think she doesn't care?" Get to know the teacher through your child. Help her to understand that her teacher has some qualities worth emulating and others that are best avoided.

What about other role models—peers, siblings, older children and adults in the community? What about the music, screen and sports personalities children may admire? How do we encourage our children to choose positive models? And how do we steer them away from the negative models—the peer who engages in self-destructive or anti-social behavior, the pop idol whose songs endorse violence against women, the local drug dealer or extortionist whose stylish clothes and fancy car may be perceived as symbols of "success"?

The good news is that if a child has high self-esteem and has had solid role modeling from parents and teachers, he can usually be counted on to resist the negative influence of peers and media celebrities. Of course a little input from you can help nudge him in the right direction.

> **Get to know who your child's role models are and reinforce his good choices.**

Know who your child's role models are. Listen and observe; pay attention to who he responds to; notice the books, records, posters and cards he collects. Look for occasions to open lines of communication about his role models. Find out what values he admires in them. *Avoid being judgmental in your response*—this is an information-gathering process, and getting preachy will only make your child less likely to be open with you. If you're pleased with his chosen role model, reinforce his choice by letting him know it. If you're not, try to refocus his attention. Buy him a tape by a group he likes whose songs *aren't* offensive to you. Identify a friend who has the positive qualities your child admires without the negative traits that bother you, and encourage your child to spend time with him.

Ultimately, you may need to exercise your parental responsibility to point your child away from negative role models. If you don't want her spending so much time with that friend who is disrespectful to adults and seems to lack motivation, if you're offended by the rock band that sports Nazi regalia, it's time to impose limits. Always be specific about *what* you object to about her role models to avoid sending the message that there is something wrong with *her* for choosing them. She may admire what she perceives as her friend's "independence," and a swastika may be nothing more to her than an antique symbol of "badness," like a pirate flag. Restrict the hours she may spend with her friend; explain to her who the Nazis were and why you don't want such symbols in your home, but leave her self-esteem intact.

With adolescence comes the third phase, when young people learn primarily through the *inspiration* of others. This is a time of heroes and heroines, when our no-longer-children single out people they admire and strive to be like them. By this time our influence as role models has been well decided. The values we have taught them through instruction and example will determine the kind of person to whom they look for inspiration—the person who contributes to the world, or the one who takes what he can get from it. By the time your children are adolescents, you can readily see what sort of role model you have been to them.

※

When Sonia was sixteen, she planned to spend the summer working as a waitress at a vacation resort. The night before she left, her father called her into his den for a little talk. Like most teenagers she saw her parents as woefully out-of-touch fossils, and she expected an embarrassing lecture on the dangers of sex, drugs and rock 'n' roll. Instead, her father said, "You're going to be facing some tough decisions over the next few months. I figure by now your values are pretty well established, and nothing I tell you is going to make much of a difference. You know what our values are. We believe we've raised you right, but we also feel confident that we've raised you to make your own judgment. Just remember that we're always here if there's anything you need to talk about. Have a great summer."

Today Sonia is 37 with a child of her own. When she thinks of her responsibility as a role model, she looks back on this incident. "I think I *do* have good values, thanks to my parents," she says. "I'm glad they didn't stifle my growth with guilt and that they gave me the freedom to make choices. But I'm glad too that they showed me what they thought was right. If I can do the same for my kids, I'll be content that I've been a good role model for them."

※

To become the best possible role model for your children, and to optimize their choice of other role models, follow the tips on the next page.

Tips for Helping Your Child Choose Positive Role Models

1. **Identify your own role models.** Think about the people you have admired and who have influenced your life. Identify the qualities that made them your role models. Tell your children about them and how they helped shape your life.

2. **Remember: you're on stage.** You are constantly modeling a role, so be careful not to muff your cues. If you want to model values, think twice before you tell a lie, run a red light, crack a joke that demeans an ethnic group, wear or display negative sayings on clothing or bumper stickers, or exhibit other behavior that sends a negative message to your children.

3. **Point out inappropriate behavior.** Don't let the negative behavior of others go by without a discreet comment to your child. The Little League coach who screams profanities at his players, the parent who yells at the coach, the authority figure who acts rudely because he can get away with it—let your child know when he or she has seen inappropriate behavior.

4. **Help every Sarah find her Lauren.** Expose your child to potential role models in his area of interest, starting with other children. Take him to a game, concert, play, etc., in which an older child he knows is participating. If possible, arrange for him to go backstage and meet the performers. Seek out adult role models too. If your daughter plays basketball, take her to a women's basketball game at a local college. See whether she can attend a practice or meet some of the players. Ask your child who are the adults he admires. If it's a neighbor, arrange for him to spend time with your child. If it's a public figure, encourage your child to read more about her in newspapers, magazines or biographies.

Nurturing Your Child's Uniqueness

Sarah's parents respected and encouraged anything that was important to her.

Do you know that your child is a star? He may only be waiting to discover his area of stardom—that quality we call *uniqueness*. Many people never discover it, and for them life remains an unfulfilled journey. For those who do recognize their unique selves, unbelievable things are possible.

One of our responsibilities as parents is to help our children find and develop this "star quality" within themselves. We start by nurturing their self-esteem through our recognition of their individual worth. The next step is to help them realize their potential. We do that by letting them discover who they are—by respecting anything that is important to them, as Sarah's parents did; by allowing them to explore themselves and their world so that they may find their uniqueness and let it flourish.

A child may express uniqueness in many ways. For your son, it may be a talent for bringing people together to work toward a common goal. For your daughter, it may be a way of solving problems. It may be a passion for a game, a craft, the world of nature. For the child of a friend of mine, it's a fascination with tap dancing. At the age of four he would watch old Gene Kelly movies on TV and do his best to imitate him. At six he was enrolled in lessons. At nine, he's often asked to perform at community functions. He feels special. He is on his way to the top— and not necessarily as a dancer. There are not enough musicals made in Hollywood, not enough dance companies in the world to provide jobs for all children with a passion for dancing. But when your child smiles at you from the stage during a dance recital, you both know that for that one instant she is a dancer. The skill you help your child develop will make her feel special and build her self-confidence. It's not necessarily the career path she will follow. It *is* a path to her self-discovery as a human being.

> *The skill you help your child develop will make her feel special and build her self-confidence.*

What is it that your child does that's just a little bit special? For that matter, what is it your child *does*? "It's a wise father who knows his child"—and that goes for mothers too. Try this little quiz on each of your children. Write your answers on a sheet of paper. Ignore the questions that don't apply. Then let your child check your answers and grade your quiz. If he's a pre-reader, go over the questions orally and make a game of it.

How Well Do You Know Your Child?

1. Who is your child's best friend?
2. What color would he like his room to be?
3. Who is (currently) your child's greatest hero?
4. What embarrasses her most?
5. What is his biggest fear?
6. What is her favorite kind of music?

Continued

Continued

7. What person outside the family has most influenced his life?

8. What are her favorite and least favorite subjects in school?

9. What is his favorite activity in gym class?

10. Of what accomplishment is your child proudest?

11. What is your child's biggest complaint about the family?

12. What is (currently) her favorite television show?

13. What sport does your child most enjoy playing or watching?

14. If he could have anything he wanted, what would he choose?

15. Who has been your child's favorite teacher?

16. What most readily makes your child angry?

17. Does your child feel liked by the children at school?

18. What would your child like to be when she grows up?

19. What has been your child's deepest disappointment this year?

20. Does your child feel too big, too small or "just right"?

21. What gift from you does your child cherish most?

22. What would be her first choice for a vacation?

23. What chore does he most dislike?

24. What non-school books has she most recently read?

25. What is his favorite family occasion?

26. What foods does she most like and dislike?

27. What nickname is he called in school?

28. When does your child prefer to do homework: right after school, after dinner, before bed or in the morning?

29. What type of animal would your child choose to have as a pet?

Helping Your Child Develop "Star Quality"

Did you "pass"? If not, maybe you'd better take some time getting to know this stranger in your house! Only then can you move beyond "who your child is" to "who your child can be."

There are many techniques you can use to discover your child's uniqueness. The most widely used might be called the "31 flavors" method—to offer your child as many choices as possible and let him pick his favorite flavor. We talked about this method back on page 28. The first step is to let your child explore as many options as possible. Swimming, hiking, volleyball, aikido, chess, dancing, ceramics, gardening, dog training, woodworking, creative writing, bird study, operating a business, astronomy, a musical instrument—the options are limitless. Even if you're on a tight budget, the abundance of available choices may surprise you. Churches, community centers, the YMCA, and recreation centers are good places to start. They offer a wide variety of classes for children. Many of them offer scholarships. The local public library can be an outstanding resource. The children's librarian can point you toward "how-to" books on subjects of potential interest, and the free "parents' papers" published in many communities are often available at the checkout counter. Don't forget to ask your child's teacher. She spends six hours a day helping your child learn and watching him choose activities. She can be a fine resource for identifying his special choices.

> *Let your child explore different activities to discover her interests.*

Because there are so many flavors to taste, begin this exploration when your child is young. If you pay close attention to how he reacts to different activities and learning situations, you will soon discover which ones he most enjoys. Be sure to let the choices be his and not yours.

Observe your child's passive interests too. With a little encouragement, passive interests can become active involvements.

In his middle-school years, Noel spent all his spare time in video arcades. One evening his father found him reading a magazine article about the young programmer who had designed one of his favorite games. "Why not write to this guy and tell him how much you like his game?" Noel's father suggested. "Maybe he'd let you in on a few secrets of how to get to the next level." Noel acted on his father's suggestion, and to his surprise, he got a reply from the designer. This young man turned out to have been a game fanatic just like Noel. At sixteen he had decided that he wanted to earn his living designing games. His programming studies had begun with a free course offered by a computer store.

For the first time, Noel began to visualize himself as a designer of video games instead of just a player. He signed up for a computer class at school. He took an after-school job to earn money to buy a computer.

After discovering your child's uniqueness, your next step is to guide him in developing it into "star quality." During this process, it is helpful to remember the lesson of Chinese bamboo. For four years

> *Nurture your child's special interests without judgment or criticism.*

after planting, the Chinese bamboo seed is watered and fertilized with great care—but nothing happens. Then during the fifth year it germinates—and within six weeks it can grow to a height of 90 feet.

The development of any talent is much like the growth of Chinese bamboo. It needs a great deal of watering, fertilizer and nurturing during its "dormant" years. Too often children quit because they can't see their talent germinating. Too often we nudge them toward quitting through our impatience or indifference. It is essential to remember that only through your love and her achievement will your child develop the self-esteem that empowers her to push on to greater achievement. Nothing will happen without care and nurturing—your encouragement and praise. Make only positive remarks about your child's efforts. Avoid judging, criticizing or comparing. Go out of your way to applaud any time her "star quality" shines even a little bit brighter, when she has been especially diligent in her practice or when she gets past a roadblock that's been holding her back. You will observe her confidence growing even while the seed of her talent remains hidden. Then will come that moment when she germinates—when she begins to identify herself as a runner, a dancer, a video-game designer. At this point she will recognize her own star quality.

From the time Alexandra learned her letters, her mother noticed how she loved to write. She would form words and even short sentences with the alphabet magnets on the refrigerator. By first grade she was writing down her own stories and poems, and the magnets were being used to display them on the refrigerator door. Her teachers too recognized her special gift and her enthusiasm for writing. One in particular gave her the chance to help her with class bulletin boards and her weekly letters home to parents. This teacher encouraged her to put her writings together in a book and let her use the school binding machine to make it a real book. A real book was evidence that she was a real writer. Alexandra went on to become the editor of her high-school newspaper and to major in journalism in college.

Here are a few more ideas to aid you in identifying and nurturing the uniqueness in your child.

Tips to Nurture Your Child's Uniqueness

1. **Make it a hundred flavors.** By now you know lots of ways to expose your child to the opportunities that are out there and to gauge her interests. Here is an ordinary one you may not have thought of: magazines. Magazines can stimulate a child's thinking and open a conversation link that lets you discover her interests and share ideas. Pay attention to the publications she picks up in the dentist's office or the supermarket. Ask neighbors and co-workers whether they subscribe to any magazines and whether they'll give you back issues to take home. If your child shows an interest, get her a subscription as a special present. Make a point of reading the issues yourself and discussing them with your child.

2. **Don't forget television.** Even the much-maligned "boob tube" can give you and your child insights into possible areas of interest. Watch her favorite shows with her and use them as springboards for discussion. What is it she admires about the characters? What interests her about the story? Look for ways to "channel" passive viewing into active achievement by suggesting goals based on her responses.

3. **Avoid the pitfall of "uncool."** If your child feels secure in her personal worthiness and has strong, positive role models, she can generally be counted on to resist peer pressure toward negative achievement. There is one sort of peer pressure, however, that is harder to resist—that which tends to regard any sign of uniqueness as "uncool." Make sure in your conversations with your child that she recognizes her uniqueness as a positive thing; that it's OK not to be like everybody

Continued

Continued

else. Role-play situations in which others put her down for having an unusual interest. Help her think of a snappy, non-negative comeback for such times; e.g., "Thanks for the compliment!"

4. **Balance involvement with restraint.** Remember, it's your *child's* uniqueness that's at issue here, not yours. Take an active hand in helping him identify his interests and develop his star quality, but don't stifle it by assuming ownership. Be willing to back off when his goals for himself are clearly different from yours or when he wishes to pursue them without your interference. Let him choose the activity that's most important to *him* without trying to steer him toward the one that's most gratifying to *you*. If his choice does happen to be in harmony with yours, that's great. Just don't be so pleased about his choice that you claim credit for it or take control of his efforts.

Build Self-Esteem Through Active Listening

He **listened attentively as she described move by move what she had done on the bars.**

Have you ever been in a conversation that turns out not to be a conversation at all? You're talking about something that's important to you when you realize that the other person isn't listening. How does it make you feel?

Now, how do you suppose your child feels when he's the one not being listened to—and the non-listener is *you*? It's certain to negatively affect his sense of personal worthiness. Think of Sarah, home from school after her triumph in the playground. Her dad took time out to listen to Sarah's account of her day. How do you suppose her performance that Saturday would have been affected if he had listened-without-listening, or if he had said, "Not now, honey, I'm busy"?

We're *always* busy. It's an inescapable condition of parenthood. We can't "be there" for our children 24 hours a day. And so it's important to truly be with them when we *are* there—to take the time to listen so that they know they count in our lives. The way to do this is through *active listening*.

"Active listening" is a phrase coined by psychologist Carl Rogers. It means showing your respect by giving your child your attention and concentration. It means making sure the child *knows* she has been heard and understood.

Active listening means your child can ask for your attention without being dismissed, shamed, judged, or denied.

It means making sure the child knows she can ask for your attention without being dismissed, shamed, judged, or denied. It means listening not only to what your child is saying but to the feelings behind the words.

Your daughter tells you that the teacher chose her poem to read aloud to the class. Which response do you think will have the most positive effect on her self-esteem: a) "That's nice, dear. Now, run along and play; Mommy's busy"; b) "I'm not surprised. I told you all you needed to do was apply yourself"; or c) "That's great. You must feel very proud. Could you read it aloud for Daddy and me at suppertime"?

Your son is being picked on by bullies. He shamefacedly tells you how they stole his lunch money for the third time that week. Which response do you think will best restore his sense of worthiness: a) "Stand up to them! Don't be a wimp!"; b) "That's too bad. Just let them be, and build up your own reputation. Eventually they'll want to become your friends"; or c) "That's hard. It makes you feel powerless, and that's a pretty awful feeling. Let's talk about different ways you might handle it"?

Your daughter is turned down by the college of her choice. You hear the dejection in her voice when she tells you the news. Which response do you think will bolster her self-esteem: a) "I told you you should have worked harder to get your math grade up"; b) "Oh, well, cheer up; it's not so bad. You can always go to the state college"; or c) "I'm sorry. I know you had your heart set on going there. Do you want to be by yourself right now, or is this an OK time to talk about possible alternatives"?

Your son has made friends with the new boy at school, the one the other children ostracize. "Tim's a good kid; he just talks too much," your son says pensively. "But he hangs around me so much that the other guys are cutting me out." Which do you think would be the most positive response: a) "I know this seems like a big deal, but believe me—in a few years you won't even remember it!"; b) "You can be Tim's friend no matter what the other kids do. I'm glad you recognize that everyone has value"; or c) "I'm proud of you for sticking with Tim. It's not easy doing the unpopular thing—even when it's the right thing"?

You probably dismissed the "a" choices right away. But what about the "b" choices? They are all "positive" responses. They indicate attentive listening—but not *active* listening. They fail to acknowledge the validity of the child's feelings: the joy of being recognized as competent, the shame of powerlessness, the disappointment of dashed hope, the dilemma between doing what is easy *vs.* doing what is right. Only the "c" responses indicate the type of listening that builds self-esteem.

How to Listen Actively to Your Children

Like most of the techniques discussed in this book, active listening is a habit that you can learn. The way to begin is by—listening. Pay attention to the way people talk to one another. (This may mean a little constructive eavesdropping.) It may shock you to discover how little people truly try to understand one another. Instead of listening, they let their mind wander or think about what they are going to say next.

Now turn the microphone around. Do you actively listen to what people are saying to you? Pay attention in particular to your conversations with your children. Do you interrupt them when they talk? Do you walk away, look at your watch or otherwise tune them out? Or do you note their tone and body language as well as their words? Do you respond to what they are saying as though it has importance and validity? Yes, it may be "childish talk," and the feelings it reflects may indicate an immature sense of what is significant. But the events that happen in their world are of prime importance to them, and to ridicule, judge, dismiss or deny their feelings strikes a blow at their self-esteem.

Listen to your responses, and consider how you would feel if the situation were reversed. You're telling a friend something that's meaningful to you, and he's sending back one of these messages:

- "Big deal!"

- "You're boring me."

- "Your troubles aren't so bad—be grateful for what you have."

- "I told you so!"

- "You made your bed, now lie in it!"

- "Cheer up—it's not so bad; don't worry about it."

- "Cheer up—don't pass along your negative mood to me."

- "It makes me uncomfortable when you talk about this. Let's change the subject."

Be attentive to what people are saying. Reflect their messages back at them to indicate that you have "read" the implied feelings. These responses may seem awkward and self-conscious at first, but remember the 21-day rule. If you practice them regularly, you will build a habit of active listening. To help form your new habit, observe these tips.

Tips for Active Listening

1. **Set the scene for active listening.** Let your child know he is free to come to you for meaningful discussion by showing your willingness to listen in everyday situations. This does *not* mean asking, "How was school today?" That one gets old very quickly. Listen to your child, and *then* ask questions that show you have been listening. If you need to ask him something to get him started, be creative. How about "Did you hear any good stories today?" or "What did you do today that was fun?" Try to come up with two new questions every day. It may help if you spark the discussion by telling your child one interesting thing that *you* did that day.

Continued

Continued

2. **Take an active interest in their world.** Review the question-naire on pages 15 and 16. Engage your child in conversation to fill in the answers you don't know. Take the responsibility for building special memories with your children. Plan at least one activity per month with each child, just you and she, doing something that she likes to do.

3. **Don't be an editor.** Preteen children are still conceptualizing the world. Their feelings, though intense, are not always based on well-informed fact. Let them share their opinions without correcting them—and be sure to thank them for sharing them. What they say is less important than how it makes them feel to know that someone values what they say.

4. **Respond with caution to a destructive opinion.** Don't lecture your child when he expresses an idea that goes against your values; e.g., "Going to church is a waste of time."; "So what if a kid takes a can of soda without paying? The store won't miss it."; "Marijuana can't hurt you." Instead, make it a learning experience. Lead him to challenge his own opinion through the recognition that his source may be unreliable or his conclusion poorly thought out. Start with, "Let's talk about that. How do you know it's so?" Then move on to, "Can you trust such a source of information? Where do you think *they* got it from?" Steer him to an alternate source—if possible, a book or magazine you have at home.

5. **Show empathy.** This does *not* mean responding to your child by saying "I know how you feel." *Show* that you understand

Continued

Continued

her feelings by responding specifically to them: "Noises at night *can* be scary, even when you know what they are. I remember when I was a little boy, I used to be scared when I heard the furnace switch on in the basement. Really! I knew it was only the furnace, but it still was scary. Sometimes I even used to cover my ears so I didn't have to hear it!..."

6. **Judge behavior, not feelings.** Accept all feelings as valid. It's behavior that can be good or bad—feelings just *are*. By all means set limits on your children's behavior, but allow them to talk out their feelings. Just let them know when the place or time is inappropriate: "This is something we should talk about privately. I'll be happy to listen to you when we get in the car"; or "I'm sorry, I'm too angry just now. Just let me calm down, and then I'll be able to give you all my attention."

Teaching Responsibility
Through Value-Based Limits

Her parents had rules, and they expected them to be followed, but they never changed them in the middle of the game.

If we could ask Sarah how her parents' attitude toward rules had influenced her "sense of somebodiness," she'd probably answer with a shrug. It's not easy for children—or for adults—to see the connection between self-esteem and personal responsibility. Accountability for our own behavior is a hallmark of a healthy self-esteem, but self-esteem alone does not bring it about. It's a connection we must nurture. *As parents, we can nurture our children's accountability for behavior through value-based limits consistently enforced—* or as Sarah put it, by setting rules and by not changing them in the middle of the game.

Responsibility is not something we can impose on our children. It can only come from within, from their own developing sense of themselves. As renowned psychotherapist Erich Fromm put it, "...responsibility, in its true sense, is an entirely voluntary act; it is my response to the needs, expressed or unexpressed, of another human being." This response comes from *personal values*—and these values, initially, must come from you.

What are the personal values that lead to responsibility? Honesty, trustworthiness, self-discipline, courage, consideration for others, cooperation, fairness, "stick-to-it-iveness"—we all pretty much agree on these values. Just how we express them, however, and the relative emphasis we place on them, can differ greatly from one family to another. Sarah gives us a pretty clear idea of her parents' value system: "...anything involving responsibility and respect.... If she neglected her homework, failed to follow through on a promise, or acted without considering the needs and rights of others, Sarah was sure to hear of it."

In my own home, an important value is respect for parents and teachers. Our children know that we will never tolerate their talking back to us or their disruptive behavior in school.

In other families, parents may tolerate a certain amount of talking back, as long as children abide by the their ultimate decisions. For these parents, the highest value may be openness in dealing with one another.

> **Communicate your values to your children.**

In short, no two families operate by the same set of values. No single value system is "the" path to personal responsibility. The important thing is to observe these two key principles:

- Be aware of what your values are and communicate them to your children.

- Clarify rules and expectations for your children that consistently reflect these values.

To observe these principles requires planning:

First, identify your own values.

Next, determine your needs as parents.

Then, establish rules and expectations for behavior based on your needs and reflecting your values.

Reinforce your child's positive behavior.

And finally, be consistent about enforcing limits.

Carry Out Your Plan for Teaching Responsibility

Identify your own values. The first step in teaching responsibility is to identify the values that you wish to instill in your children. This means taking a long, hard look at your values and the extent to which you live by them. Remember, past a certain age your children will emulate the behavior they *observe*, not the values you verbally endorse, no matter what limits you may set. Together, as Mom and Dad, you must work out a clear agreement about the values you wish your children to live by. These values apply whether or not Mom and Dad live under the same roof. Your children have the right not to be expected to observe two different value systems. Only if you have sole responsibility for your children can you go by your values alone.

> "I value honesty. I want our home to be a place where we are honest with one another. I want my children to share this value also."

> "I value respect for others. I want my child to understand that respecting the rights of others is important."

> "I value cooperation. I want my children to learn that we are a family that counts on one another so that each of us can do our best and be happy and secure."

Once you have examined your own values, you can more comfortably decide on rules or expectations based on those values. Parents living in separate households can develop these rules independently, as long as they agree on value-based goals for their children's behavior.

Establish your needs as parents. Before you set rules and expectations for your child you must identify the behaviors you need for your home to operate within your comfort level. Clarifying and specifying those needs will make it possible for you to establish clear behavior goals.

These needs fall into four categories: physical needs, social needs, safety needs and responsibility needs.

Physical needs. These are the factors that contribute to an orderly environment for family living. Be thorough and specific when you consider your needs for such order.

For example: Are you uncomfortable with dishes left indefinitely in the sink? If you don't really care, don't worry; they'll most likely get done sometime. If you do care, however, cleaning up after dinner may be an important expectation you have for your child.

Does it drive you crazy when your teenager's room is in a constant state of disarray? Some parents believe a child's room is his or her own space and shouldn't be interfered with. Others, however, feel that even one's own bedroom is part of the home and should be meet the "cleanliness" standards of the rest of the household.

Other physical needs you have might include: Vacuum the house each Saturday; Empty the clothes dryer; Take out the garbage each night.

Social needs. These needs relate to the interaction among family members and between family members and others. For example: Are you uncomfortable about your children squabbling over TV time? If this behavior does not promote the harmony you want, then you need to let your children know exactly what you expect. Does swearing offend you? How about sullenness at meals? About refusal to share? What are the specific "social sins" of your value system?

Social needs might include: No swearing; No borrowing someone else's things without permission; Say "please" and "thank you" to one another when appropriate.

Safety needs. Most parents find it easy to establish rules that relate to children's safety. Many are cut-and-dried issues that ensure a child's health and well-being.

Your safety needs might include: My child may not cross the street without an adult; My child may not answer the door if I'm not at home; My child may not cook on the stove when I'm not at home; My child must be home by 6:00 each day.

Your requirements for a safe living environment are important to spell out and communicate.

Responsibility needs. These needs have to do with the obligations of each child to the family and to others. Very often these are the needs that are most closely related to values. Are you uncomfortable when your children resist doing their chores? When older siblings fail to look after younger ones? When a child fails to follow through on a promise to a neighbor? When communicating expectations to your child be specific about the behavior your value system cannot accommodate.

Clarify your expectations for behavior. Once you have honestly examined your own needs, you can more confidently establish rules and expectations for your child.

If you don't want dirty dishes sitting around (and you'd like to promote a little more cooperation in your home) an appropriate expectation might be "Michelle clears the table and rinses the dished each night. Bradley loads the washer and takes out the trash."

If your child's messy room is intolerable to you, and you feel that respecting your wishes regarding your home is important, a reasonable rule might be, "Each day before school, your bed is to be made and clothes put away."

Depending on your situation, you will need to establish different expectations for each child, based on age appropriateness and the particular challenges the child's behavior poses to your needs.

Note: If your goal is to improve specific problem behaviors, keep this in mind: Don't try to change *all* your children's behaviors at once. Like so much else you've read about in this book, managing behavior is a matter of changing habits. Your children will much more readily learn new habits a few at a time than all at once. Limit your rules to five at any one time. Once your child is consistently following one of the rules, add another to the list. Keep the plan fluid in response to changing situations.

Reinforce your child's positive behavior. It's easy to notice when children aren't behaving appropriately. After all, inappropriate behavior usually irritates or inconveniences us. But ironically it's even easier to let *appropriate* behavior go unnoticed. Appropriate behavior doesn't make waves or cause our adrenaline to start racing.

Unfortunately, this is very often the reason children do not consistently make good behavior choices: No one pays any attention when they do!

The best way to guide your child toward making appropriate, responsible choices—and meeting your expectations—is to reinforce his or her positive behavior. And the best way to reinforce positive behavior is through your own praise.

In *Assertive Discipline for Parents*, educator Lee Canter emphasizes, "Effective parents are aware of the enormous impact their praise can have and will utilize it not only to build their children's self-esteem, but to help them learn appropriate behavior. Praise is the most useful positive reinforcer you possess. Your children's emotional well-being and self-confidence are directly related to the feedback they receive from you. The more positive your responses, the better they can and will feel."

Never underestimate the power of your positive attention.

> "Alexis, you said 'thank you' to Joe when he held the door for you. That was so thoughtful! And Joe, holding the door for Alexis when her hands were full of books was very considerate. You both are a pleasure to be around!"

Establish clear consequences for inappropriate behavior. If you are going to have well-defined rules and expectations you need to know how you will respond when rules are broken or expectations are not met. Taking away privileges for inappropriate behavior is an effective way for parents to teach children to accept responsibility for their actions. Children will learn that they have a choice: They can choose to follow the rules or they will choose to lose privileges. The choice is theirs.

Also, knowing in advance how *you* will respond to misbehavior will keep you from reacting emotionally and in anger. It will also help you be consistent.

> "Your curfew is 10:00 P.M. If you are not home by 10:00, you will not be allowed to go out the following weekend."

> "Dishes are to be done right after dinner. If you don't do the dishes right after dinner you will lose telephone privileges the rest of the evening."

Discuss both your expectations *and* potential consequences with your children. Ask for their input—they may have some very good suggestions. Explain also that you have these expectations because you want them to grow into responsible people who feel good about themselves and who demonstrate caring to others.

Be consistent. Nothing is less conducive to teaching responsibility, or more unfair to a child, than being indifferent to limits one week and enforcing them to the letter the next—"changing the rules in the middle of the game." If you're going to set limits, you must be firm and on-the-spot in your response when children exceed them, even when it's inconvenient for you.

❧

Alys worked evenings. She had three children, each of whom was assigned certain chores to do before bedtime. The middle child, Mary, had a habit of neglecting her chores. Alys had discussed with Mary her responsibility to the family. She did not have a choice about whether or not she did her chores— it was her job. If on occasion Mary had extra homework or some other special circumstances, she could discuss it with Alys ahead of time and arrange for a trade-off with her sister or brother, but the chores must be done.

On this particular evening, there were no special circumstances. Mary was expected to do the laundry, including sorting and folding. When Alys came home at 11:30, she found all the laundry jumbled up in a basket in front of the TV set— and Mary in bed asleep.

The next morning Alys got Mary up a half hour early.

"Mary, it's time to get up," Alys said to her daughter.

"Is it morning already? I'm so tired." Mary said sleepily."

"Yes, it's very early in the morning. And it's time to do your chores from last night."

Needless to say, Mary was not a "happy camper," and Alys had to lose a little sleep herself to enforce her rules. But it was the last time Mary neglected her chores—and her sister and brother learned too that their mother was consistent in her expectations.

⸎

As your children's behavior habits change, you'll find yourself spending less time on enforcement. Your children will be assuming responsibility for their own actions. It's the same concept as the rewards you hand out for goal attainment. Just as achievement in time becomes its own reward, so does responsibility. If your child develops habits of high self-esteem and value-based behavior, self-motivated accountability will follow. By providing a sense of direction through limits and consistency, you guide your child in developing his own sense of direction. By basing your limits on your value system, you guide him toward developing and living by his own values. By showing your growing confidence in his reliability, you help him build self-reliance.

Here are a few more things you can do to speed the process.

Tips for Teaching Your Child Responsibility Through Value-Based Limits

Introduce new responsibilities gradually. Help your children get used to personal responsibility by introducing it in small doses. They can start when they are quite young by attending to their personal hygiene on a daily basis. Then give them ever-increasing responsibilities as their maturity level suggests.

For example:

- First, a child is given the responsibility of feeding the dog every day.

Continued

- Later, when the child handles that responsibly, he or she is given the job of taking the dog for a walk every afternoon.

- Finally, having demonstrated his or her responsibility, the child is given permission to take care of the neighbors' dog while they are on vacation.

Or:

- First, a child is allowed to stay home alone for 30 minutes while the parents are visiting across the street.

- Later, the child is allowed to stay home alone for an hour while the parents are at the grocery store.

- In time, the child is allowed to stay home without a sitter while the parents go to the movies.

- Finally, the child is given permission to babysit for a child in the neighborhood.

Place your children in situations of responsibility. Show your confidence by allowing them to assume responsibilities outside your supervision. Giving a child full care of a pet is one classic technique. Another, when the child's age and your budget allow it, is to send her to camp. She'll be getting to the breakfast table on time each morning dressed and ready for the day without you being there to motivate her.

Never argue with your child. Arguing should cease to be a part of your style of communicating with your children. Be consistent and back up your rules and expectations with action, but don't let your child engage you in argument. Just state what you want and restate it if necessary. Use the words "I understand" when you restate your demands:

Continued

Continued

Child: I don't want to do my homework. I want to watch this show.

Parent: I understand, but it's time to do homework.

Child: You're so unfair. I never get to see this.

Parent: I understand, but homework is your responsibility and I expect you to do it now.

Child: I only have a little to do, and it's stupid anyway. Can I do it in front of the TV?

Parent: Chris, turn off the TV and begin your homework right now.

Repeat as often as necessary. (Psychologists call this the *broken record* technique.) You remain calm and confident while your child learns that you mean what you say, that arguing will get him nowhere, and that he might as well get on with his life.

Model responsible behavior. If you want your child to learn responsibility, show her what it means. If you start a project at home, complete it—even if the end result isn't exactly what you had in mind. Take your child to work with you and let her observe what "doing a job" means. In all situations, let your own behavior reflect the values you want hers to reflect.

Don't lose sight of love. Don't impose responsibility at the expense of your child's self-esteem. Always remember when setting and enforcing limits to let your unconditional love for your child shine through. Place limits on your child's unacceptable behavior—not on his sense of self.

Demonstrating Responsibility Toward Others

It was funny how feeling
good about herself made her want to do things for other
people...and the other way around too.

"Every 'U' is an 'I,'" said a bumper sticker of some years ago. To recognize the essential worthiness of others is the truest sign of a successful person. Only when we have adequate self-esteem can we rise above the anxious condition of "looking out for number one" and give others the care and attention they need for their own success. Yet as Sarah knew, it works both ways. Doing things for others can raise our own self-esteem. It's an illustration of another popular saying: "What goes around comes around."

Of course it's more than "doing things for others." It's a recognition that every human being has value and significance. It's a sense of *responsibility* to others and to the world in which we live. It's an expression of *respect* in the truest sense of the word—respect for the differences among human beings and for the basic worthiness of all. It's an affirmation of *faith*, of the relationship between one's self and the universe outside one's self; a spiritual energy source that acknowledges the sacredness of life whether we express it in traditional religious belief or simply as an appreciation of the oneness of the universe. It's a blueprint for *caring*, for seeking ways of dealing with family members, friends, acquaintances and strangers alike in ways that acknowledge their freedom, their dignity, their essential humanness.

Wouldn't it be wonderful if everyone's self-esteem allowed room for such responsibility and respect...such *caring*? We would need no laws and no jails. When people do not respect themselves, it is impossible for them to respect others. But like personal responsibility, "other-directed" responsibility does not proceed automatically from self-esteem—it must be nurtured. It's a skill that the adult community must model for its youth.

The trouble is that most of us just aren't doing the job. We've heard it said that our country faces a "crisis of caring." Studies of school dropouts indicate that their most common complaint about their teachers is, "They don't care." Instead of caring, we adopt an approach to social problem-solving

> *Contributing to the success of others fuels our own success as well.*

summed up by the phrase "just say no." It lets us absolve ourselves of any responsibility and dismiss from our concern anyone who lacks the strength of character (i.e., the self-esteem) to say no.

As parents, we need to establish guidelines by which our children learn how to contribute to the success of others instead of saying "it's not my problem." Like Sarah, they'll discover that it fuels their own success as well.

Teaching Other-Directed Responsibility

The foundation for any child's sense of responsibility to others is the family unit. As parents, we need to teach our children by instruction and example such values as sharing, working together toward common goals, respectful listening and mutual support—i.e., building one another's self-esteem by encouraging their successes instead of downgrading it through belittlement or teasing.

Of course you would never willfully encourage selfishness in your children. You would certainly never tolerate cruelty by one child to another, or to a neighbor. But what behavior do you model regarding other-directed responsibility when you:

- push ahead to be first in line at the supermarket or speed up to beat a red light in traffic?

- grab the last piece of chicken at dinner?

- call children by "putdown" nicknames such as "slowpoke" or "half pint"—even affectionately?

- speak demeaningly of any racial, religious or national group?

- try to get a laugh at someone else's expense?

- display a lack of caring toward people in need of help?

In brief: If we want our children to have respect for the worth and dignity of others, we must be diligent and conscientious about modeling such respect until it becomes—you guessed it—a *habit*.

At times this value may be in conflict with other values. A child may feel that it impinges on her rights of privacy and personal choice to have to "show respect on demand." At such times a parent must take on the role of wise counselor, finding compromises that preserve the self-esteem of all concerned.

✦✦✦✦✦

Seven-year-old Josh was delighted with his Christmas present, a wall calendar with photos from the "Star Trek" TV show. Josh's ten-year-old sister, Diana, was a Star Trek fan too and was eager to have a look at the calendar; but Josh, who rarely had the opportunity to exercise power over his older sister, gleefully refused to let her see it.

Diana came in tears to her father, Jim. "I don't understand why he has to be so *mean*," she said. "All I want to do is look at it. He knows I love Star Trek. If it were my present, I'd let *him* see it!"

"I understand," Jim said. "I know your feelings are hurt. But Josh has a right to do what he wants with his own things. I'm sorry."

Diana was unsatisfied by this response. But then Jim knocked on his son's door. "Josh, is there some reason you don't want your sister to see your new calendar?" he said.

Josh shrugged.

"It's your present and you can do what you want with it," Jim said, "But I know you care about other people's feelings, and right now Diana is very unhappy."

Josh went back to his room. An hour later, Jim heard his children chattering happily together over the calendar.

***

When family members have the habit of treating each other with respect and caring, it's a small step to extend such behavior to the wider community. Once again, we as parents must model the behavior for our children. Our choices are wide, and we may choose as our values and opportunity allow.

"Charity" is a pillar of many religious traditions. Jews and Christians are taught to "tithe"; to set aside a portion of their income (literally a tenth) for the poor. Muslims are taught that providing for one's less-fortunate neighbors takes precedence over the pilgrimage to Mecca. Whether charitable acts come from a religious impulse or from an appreciation of one's self as a part of the human

> *Negative reinforcers form a child's negative feelings about himself.*

community, parents can make them a family project. Sit down together and have everyone participate in deciding to whom to give a family contribution. Have everyone pledge something significant. For younger children, it might be a quarter out of their allowance; for older ones, the price of some desired toy or treat they were planning to buy for themselves.

Many families join volunteers at shelters for the homeless, distributing dinners at Thanksgiving and Christmas. Make this a family project—and don't limit yourselves to the holidays! Such institutions are always in need of volunteers to assist in such tasks as cleaning up or helping transients fill out papers. Your children will better appreciate the positive feelings that come from helping others if it's not just a one-time occasion.

Many volunteer organizations conduct walk-a-thons to raise money.

Participate as a family in a walk-a-thon of your choice, or organize one.

Working for a healthy planet offers a variety of other-directed goals. In a community where we used to live, the local nature center held an annual Community Clean-Up Day. Adults and children of all ages would pick up trash bags at a central location, then fan out through the community picking up bits of refuse. The trash bags were placed alongside the road for pickup by the sanitation department, and all the hard-working volunteers would celebrate with a barbecue. Find out if such a program exists in your community. If not, why not start one?

With your help and encouragement, even very young children can catch the spirit of caring and responsibility to others.

⌘

When Rachel was in kindergarten, her class learned about endangered species. She and her friend Monica decided they wanted to help save whales and other endangered animals. The two girls picked tangerines from the tree in Rachel's backyard and put them in a basket. Escorted by Rachel's father, they knocked on neighbors' doors and asked them if they wanted to help save the animals by buying a few tangerines. They earned $3.25 that day, which they sent (again with Dad's help) with a letter to the National Wildlife Federation. Three weeks later, they received a formal letter of thanks. Seven years later, Rachel is still on the NWF's mailing list and continues to make contributions.

⌘

Visiting a retirement home, volunteering with the Humane Society, participating in the Adopt-a-Highway program, having your child help you take an elderly neighbor grocery shopping, donating clothes, toys or books to charity; bringing a "welcome basket" to a new neighbor, working with children at a day-care center—the list of possibilities for family participation in other-directed activities is endless. Here are a few additional things you might do to encourage such a spirit of participation in your children.

Tips for Family Projects to Help Others

1. **Encourage sharing.** This concept tends to be more difficult for "only children" or for those widely spaced in age. Children from large families have to learn at an early age to share parents, toys, even clothes. Create situations that will encourage children to share. Join with other parents in setting up play groups; organize block parties or family gatherings where children are brought together. When children learn early to share with one another, they will more readily appreciate the concept of sharing with the wider community.

2. **Plan and encourage group activities.** Family game nights, team sports, and community activities such as scouting or singing in a choir can help children learn and experience the give and take of cooperation with others. Family vacations or outings can be great teaching tools. Let the children have a say in the plan: where to go, how much time to spend there, what they want to see and do. Make sure the excursion includes something for everyone.

3. **Start a family recycling program.** Recycling is a great way for children to start developing an awareness of being a part of a wider community. In many locations, there can be the incentive of a cash "reward" as well. As a family activity, organize the recycling of cans, glass, plastic and paper. Divide and share responsibilities based on age appropriateness.

Social Skills: Putting On the Aspect of Success

Sarah **took it as a compliment. She thanked them for their words of congratulations. They made her feel special.**

I once saw an entire second-grade classroom burst into spontaneous applause. The occasion was a boy being the first in the class to be called up by the teacher to receive his report card. The child was taken by surprise, but he smiled and thanked the class for their congratulations. Like Sarah, he was made to feel special by his classmates' approval—it confirmed his promotion to the third grade as a real achievement—and his gracious response returned the positive feeling back at them. As the roll of names continued, the children applauded as each was called.

Why was this incident so remarkable? Because so many people lack the self-esteem to accept a compliment with a sincere smile and a "thank you." When they hear something good about themselves, they feel like impostors. You tell a friend you like the dress she's wearing, and she responds, "Oh, this old rag? I've had it for years." It's embarrassing—you wish you hadn't opened your mouth. You make a sincere, positive statement, and you get back negative feelings in return.

Giving and receiving compliments, introducing yourself, apologizing, sharing, expressing feelings, dealing with authority—all such social skills seem to be in decline these days. Walk through almost any school and observe young people interacting with one another and with their teachers. A fourth-grade boy comes running down the hallway into his teacher's path. "Stop running!" the teacher calls. "Don't hassle me!" the child responds, sidestepping her to yell at his classmate down the hall, "Keep your ___ing hands out of my locker!"

We've become careless about social skills. We're self-conscious and suspicious about them. We regard them as tools of insincere and manipulative

> **Good social skills contribute to our inner feeling of self-worth.**

people, like Eddie Haskell on the old "Leave It to Beaver" show. In fact, such skills serve a vital function. Besides smoothing the way to successful interactions with others, they contribute to an *aspect of success* by building habits of respect and positiveness—and by now you know all about the power of such habits. When we make a habit of receiving compliments with a smile and a "thank you," we affirm the things people are saying about us, and we pass along the positive feelings to others. In this way, all such seemingly external skills contribute to our inner feeling of self-worth.

Unfortunately, the reverse is not necessarily true. High self-esteem does not automatically turn a child into a gracious individual. We can send a child off to her first day of school secure in our love and confident in her ability to set and achieve goals. Yet if she lacks social skills, we may be sending her off as a self-centered human being, disrespectful of peers and adults and generally unpleasant to be around. Fortunately, there's a place where she can acquire such skills—your home.

Creating an Aspect of Success

By now you're well acquainted with the not-so-magic formula for teaching your children new habits:

- **Teach** them the behavior you want them to display.
- **Model** the behavior at every opportunity.
- **Reward** them for the behavior with a verbal pat on the back.

Teaching social skills follows exactly the same procedure. You've already started on the basics—assuming your children know how to say "please" and "thank you." It probably took several weeks of conscientious reminding ("What do we say?") and self-conscious modeling ("Honey, will you please pass the syrup?") to effectively teach them this "level 1" social skill, but chances are they did learn it. Just apply the same procedures to the other skills you wish them to learn:

- **Tell** them how to do it.

- **Show** them by example.

- **Praise** them privately when you see them exhibit the desired behavior—and do it on a regular and consistent basis until the behavior becomes an unselfconscious act for them.

If you want your child to learn to accept compliments graciously, make a point of smiling and saying "Thank you" when someone compliments you.

If you want your child to make a favorable impression when meeting people, teach him to shake hands when introducing himself, look the person in the eye and say "It's nice to meet you"—and then make sure you model the behavior for him.

Teaching your children social skills requires a commitment to diligently practice your own.

If you want your child to be a polite conversationalist, model the behavior in your conversations with others. Look at the person who's talking to you; listen without interrupting, drifting away or mentally planning what you're going to say next; and comment without changing the subject.

If you want your child to know how to apologize graciously, make sure you show him by example when *you* are in the wrong. Look at your child when you apologize to him. Make a specific statement about the behavior you regret, offer an alternate way for responding in the future, and ask for acceptance: "Jim, I'm sorry I disciplined you in front of your friends. I know I was insensitive to your feelings, and from now on I'll 'keep it in the family' when we discuss these issues. Are we okay about this?"

In other words, teaching your children social skills requires a commitment on your part to diligently practice your own.

Perhaps the social skill that most contributes to a child's aspect of success is the skill of supporting one another within the family unit. Such support can be as varied as helping each other with homework, watching Mom compete in her bowling-league tournament, making a "You Are Special" card when someone is feeling down or celebrating the attainment of a family member's goal.

If your child feels that your home is warm and friendly and caring, a place where family members gain strength from one another, a place where she really *likes* to be, she's on her way toward becoming a successful adult. She'll know how to be caring because she's grown up in an atmosphere of caring. She'll know how to make others feel that they make a difference in the world because she comes from a home in which everyone is made to feel that they make a difference. She'll project a generosity of spirit toward others because she'll feel secure and confident enough about her own worthiness. She'll be a success not only because she sets and achieves goals but because she presents a face to the world that says "Here comes a successful person."

Here are a few ways you can help your children shape such an aspect for themselves.

Tips for Helping Your Children Create an Aspect of Success

1. **Have a no-putdown family policy.** Name-calling, "cutting" remarks, making someone the object of ridicule—such verbal abuse degrades people's self-esteem and should have no place in the family setting. Make clear to your children that no such putdowns will be tolerated. They are hurtful, and there is nothing funny about them. Enforce your ban with appropriate consequences; e.g., no TV, extra chores, "grounding."

2. **Carry no grudges.** An issue of contention that isn't resolved

Continued

Continued

can become a toxic cloud of resentment that poisons relations between family members. Make it a rule in your household never to go to bed without resolving such issues. The surest way to clear the air is through sincere forgiveness. Instead of carrying over an attitude that says "You owe me one," cancel the emotional debt. The ability to forgive those you care about the most will give strength to your family and empower you to start each new day fresh.

3. **Use family time to build constructive feelings.** Meals, weekend outings, or planned meetings are a fine forum for expressing family concerns. These are occasions to air negative feelings between family members and to rechannel them into productive feelings. Parents need to be role models in such situations. Bring up matters that are concerning you, and draw in the children with questions directed to them individually. These are occasions for you to model active listening. Question, listen, and restate their answers in a way that expresses your understanding of their feelings and your empathy.

4. **Transmit hope.** The most effective way you can provide for your children has nothing to do with financial security. It's to transmit hope, the essence of the human spirit. To have hope means to know in our heart that we have the power to make things better, that even with a loss there is a gain because it creates a place in our life for something new. Help your children approach difficult problems by restating them as challenges to be overcome. And always provide support in times of adversity. If your children can't depend on having your shoulder to cry on when they're discouraged, where else can they turn?

Your Children's Success:
Fitting the Pieces Together

Sarah was a success—she had accomplished her goal. And the two people who meant most to her in all the world had been there to see her do it.

When Sarah dismounted the bars that Saturday morning, she had just completed an ordinary week. Yet in terms of personal growth, it was anything but ordinary. She had set a goal that was to her an expression of her uniqueness and worthiness as a human being. She had achieved her goal in the presence of the parents whose love and encouragement had first given her that sense of worthiness. She had enlisted the help of an admired other and given herself a boost of self-confidence through mental practice. She had experienced a surge of positive feeling as a result of her accomplishment and spontaneously shared it with others. She had increased her personal store of self-esteem, a "bank account" she would later be able to draw on for future successes.

Raising our children—guiding the next generation and those to come—is the most important job we do. We all want our children to be successful—to grow up to be independent, self-fulfilling adults who find satisfaction in their achievements, take responsibility for their actions and help others along their paths to success as well. This book has given you an overview of how you can guide your children toward developing the qualities of success we listed back on pages 12 and 13.

Children Who Are Bound for Success

By knowing themselves to be goal setters and achievers, by appreciating their own uniqueness, by acknowledging that they have control over their lives and by choosing positive role models, they will develop a sense of **direction** about their lives.

By feeling secure in their worthiness as human beings, by having the skills to erase doubt through visualization and self-talk and by maintaining a **positive** mental attitude, they will approach life's challenges with enthusiasm and persistence.

From experiencing success and by compiling such experiences into their overall concept of themselves, they will have the **self-confidence** to take risks and shrug off setbacks.

Through the self-discipline acquired by setting and achieving goals and from living in a family that balances unconditional love with value-based limits, they will develop a sense of personal **responsibility**.

From the personal validation that comes from being listened to and appreciated, through the confidence that comes from their sense of competence and from their recognition of the worth of others, they will become effective **communicators**.

Because of their positive approach to life and their sense of other-directed responsibility, they will grow into **caring** people who help others achieve success.

From their perception of themselves as unique and worthy individuals and through an appreciation of their relationship to the universe outside themselves, they will develop and nurture strong **spiritual values**.

In short, they'll be children with high self-esteem—children who can look at themselves and say, "I am really an OK kid!"

These qualities of success that I wanted for my own children—and want now for my grandchildren—are like pieces of a jigsaw puzzle. As parents it is our responsibility to fit these pieces carefully together to form a whole child. Unlike the puzzles you can put together on a card table over a weekend, this one takes a lifetime to complete. We need to think about each aspect and component of self-esteem as an individual piece of this puzzle, visualize how they will all fit together, and then begin our job.

During your assembly of this unique puzzle, do not lose sight of those seemingly insignificant events like Sarah's challenge on the bars. It is such events that require your special attention, and they happen every day. The little things you do and say to your child all contribute to the big picture, just as the subtle curves and color patterns in the jigsaw puzzle make it fit together.

It's been said before, but it's worth saying again: It's the hardest job you will ever love.